Crafts for Kids Who Are Wild
·······ABOUT·······
THE WILD

CRAFTS
for Kids Who Are Wild About the
WILD

By Kathy Ross
Illustrated by Sharon Lane Holm

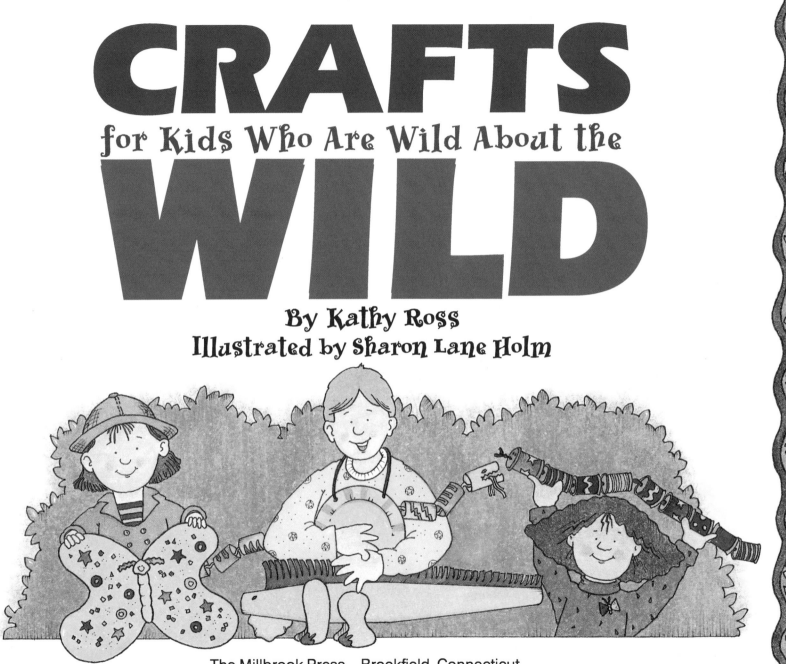

The Millbrook Press   Brookfield, Connecticut

For Jean, the editor we are wild about.
K.R. and S.L.H.

Library of Congress Cataloging-in-Publication Data
Ross, Kathy (Katharine Reynolds), 1948–
Crafts for kids who are wild about the wild / by Kathy Ross: illustrated by
Sharon Lane Holm.
p.   cm.
Summary: Provides instructions for more than seventy-five simple craft
projects involving dinosaurs, ocean animals, polar animals, insects, reptiles,
and animals of the rain forest and desert.
ISBN 0-7613-0440-1
1. Handicraft—Juvenile literature.   2. Animals in art—Juvenile literature.
3. Plants in art—Juvenile literature. [1. Animals in art.   2. Handicraft.]
I. Holm, Sharon Lane, ill. II. Title.
TT160.R714227   1998
745.5—dc21   98-17334   CIP   AC

Published by The Millbrook Press, Inc.
2 Old New Milford Road
Brookfield, Connecticut 06804

The crafts are selected from *Crafts for Kids Who Are Wild About Dinosaurs,*
Crafts for Kids Who Are Wild About Oceans, Crafts for Kids Who Are Wild
About Polar Regions, Crafts for Kids Who Are Wild About Rainforests, Crafts
for Kids Who Are Wild About Insects, Crafts for Kids Who Are Wild About
Deserts, and *Crafts for Kids Who Are Wild About Reptiles* by Kathy Ross

Introduction

There are certain children who like to make things: Children who may or may not show any particular talent in art but who still love to create; children who are better able to understand the world around them when they try to copy it in bits and pieces of found materials; children who look creatively at the things around them and try to turn them into something else; children who find joy in the very process of re-creating. I was one of those children.

This book contains craft projects organized into seven natural history topics, some grouped by species and others by environment. Directions are given for creating models of a wide variety of plant and animal species in many different ways in the hope of appealing to as many creative and learning styles as possible. The projects include not only somewhat elaborate models appropriate for use in science projects but also functional and decorative items and even games. One of you might be fascinated by the Flashing Firefly Puppet built around a flashlight, while another will want to make the Lucky Ladybug Necklace. One may want to build a Giant Apatosaurus Model, while another will enjoy making and using an Oasis Stamp Licker. Whatever project you choose, in whatever form or for whatever purpose, the process of re-creating something will offer both understanding of the subject and pleasure in creative work.

Creating these projects offer fun and satisfaction, but it is my hope and intention that doing so will be a springboard to a search for more information. To that end, following each section, I have included a list of books for further reading.

So join me in the fun of being "wild" about the wild.

Kathy Ross

Contents

Dinosaurs

Whether you are just learning about dinosaurs or are already fascinated by them, you will enjoy this section, which contains eleven projects related to prehistoric times. You can build a Giant Apatosaurus Model for a science project, or make yourself a Parasaurolophus Mask for Halloween. Decorate your room with Dinosaur Window Scenes—or impress your teacher with a Pasta Fossil Plaque.

There is lots of room for your own creativity when working with dinosaurs. Remember that no one really knows what color the dinosaurs were, so when a project calls for paint, you can decide for yourself the color or colors you will use.

There are loads of great books about dinosaurs available. I've listed some of my favorites on page 32.

Pasta Fossil Plaque

Here is what you need:

potting soil
white glue
pasta in different shapes
Styrofoam tray
bowl and spoon
measuring cup
scissors
felt

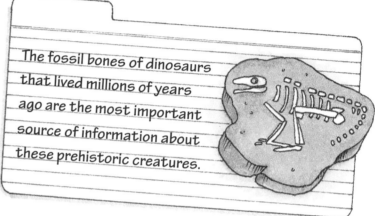

The fossil bones of dinosaurs that lived millions of years ago are the most important source of information about these prehistoric creatures.

Here is what you do:

Mix one cup of potting soil with just enough white glue to hold the dirt together. Shape the dirt into a ball and set it on the Styrofoam tray. Press the ball down until it is flat and about ½ inch (1.5 centimeters) thick.

10

2) Pasta shapes make great "bones." Arrange different pasta shapes to design your own fossil—the possibilities are endless! When you have a design you like, carefully arrange it on top of the gluey dirt. Gently press the pasta into the dirt to make sure it will stay. Cover the pasta with a layer of glue. Let the dirt dry on the Styrofoam tray until it is hard. This could take two or three days.

3) When the dirt is dry, cut a piece of felt to fit the bottom of the plaque. Glue the felt on the bottom of the dirt plaque to keep the plaque from scratching the surface you place it on.

Make a fossil plaque for someone you know who is wild about dinosaurs.

Giant Apatosaurus Model

Here is what you need:

large oatmeal box with lid
six cardboard paper-towel tubes
two cardboard toilet-tissue tubes
two apple seeds
sharp, black permanent marker
sixteen elbow macaroni
large mixing bowl and spoon
measuring cup
white glue
scissors
old, dark-colored T-shirt
large Styrofoam or plastic-covered tray
cellophane tape

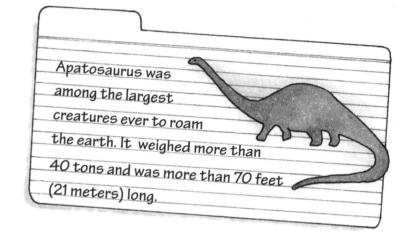

Apatosaurus was among the largest creatures ever to roam the earth. It weighed more than 40 tons and was more than 70 feet (21 meters) long.

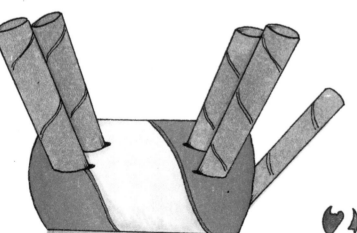

Here is what you do:

1 Turn the oatmeal box on its side. This will be the body of the dinosaur. To make the legs, draw four circles on the underside of the body, two at each end. Use the end of one of the paper-towel tubes as a pattern. Cut inside the traced circle so that the legs will be a tight fit. Insert a paper-towel tube into each of the four holes. If the hole is too small to get the tube through, just keep trimming small pieces from the edge of the hole until the tube fits.

2 To make the tail, cut a hole in the back of the dinosaur (one of the flat ends of the oatmeal box). Slide a paper-towel tube in the hole at an angle so that it points downward, just like a tail.

12

3) Cut a slit about three quarters of the way up the side of one of the toilet-tissue tubes. Wrap the two cut edges of the tube around each other to form a cone. Tape the cone shape to hold it securely in place. Slide the round end of the tube into the end of the dinosaur tail so that the cone sticks out and the tail is pointed.

4) Cut a hole in the front of the dinosaur (the other flat end of the oatmeal box). Push in a paper-towel tube at an angle so that it points upward to form the dinosaur's neck.

5) Cut a slit in a toilet-tissue tube about one third of the way up the side. Wrap the two cut edges around each other to form a cone. Tape the cone shape to secure it. Slide the round end of the tube into the end of the neck. Tip the point of the cone forward to form the head of the dinosaur.

6) Cut the old T-shirt into pieces that will be large enough to cover all the parts of the dinosaur. In a large bowl, mix $1\frac{1}{2}$ cups (375 milliliters) of glue with $\frac{3}{4}$ cup (185 milliliters) of water. Soak each of the shirt pieces in the glue so that they are completely wet.

7 Cover the legs, tail, and head of the dinosaur with the gluey fabric. Cover the body last. Rub the dinosaur with glue to make the model sturdier and to hold down any loose edges of the fabric. Stand the dinosaur on a Styrofoam tray to dry.

8 When the dinosaur is dry, glue four elbow macaroni to each foot for claws. Draw a dot in the middle of each apple seed with the marker and glue the seeds on the dinosaur's head for eyes.

Scientists believe that Apatosaurus moved in large herds and ate huge amounts of vegetation as they traveled. If you make your own herd of these giants, you will want to make lots of Necktie Trees to feed them!

Necktie Tree

Here is what you need:

long cardboard wrapping-paper tube, about 2 inches
(5 centimeters) in diameter
masking tape
twelve old neckties
scissors
white glue
paintbrush and green and brown poster paint
newspaper to work on

Here is what you do:

Cut the tube so that it is about 22 inches
(55 centimeters) long. Cover the outside of
the tube in a random pattern with pieces of masking
tape that are 1 inch (2.5 centimeters) square. It is
easiest to tear off a long strip of tape first and then
tear the smaller pieces off that strip. The tape will give
the tube a rough, scaly look, like the bark of a tree.

Paint the tree trunk brown and let it dry.

Cut a piece 10 inches (25 centimeters) long
from the thin end of each necktie. Rub glue
around the top inside edge of the tree trunk and tuck
the cut ends of the tie pieces into the top of the tree.
Arrange the tie leaves so that they drape around the
top of the tree.

Paint the leaves green and let them dry.

Stand one or more of these trees
near a hungry plant-eating dinosaur.

Tree ferns provided food for many of the dinosaurs.

Parasaurolophus Mask

Here is what you need:

12-inch by 14-inch (30-centimeter by 36-centimeter)
   poster board in color of your choice
tissue paper of same color as poster board
cardboard wrapping-paper tube, about 1 inch
   (2.5 centimeters) in diameter
paper party horn
masking tape
white glue
scissors
bowl
pencil
hole punch
string
newspaper to work on
Styrofoam trays

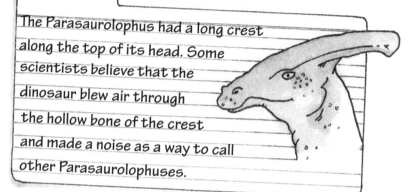

The Parasaurolophus had a long crest along the top of its head. Some scientists believe that the dinosaur blew air through the hollow bone of the crest and made a noise as a way to call other Parasaurolophuses.

Here is what you do:

Overlap the two bottom corners of the narrow side of the poster board to form a cone, leaving an opening at the end. Tape the overlapping edges together. Hold the poster board in front of your face like a mask, with your chin firmly in the cone-shaped end. On the front of the mask, gently mark in pencil where you should cut the eye holes. Remove the mask from your face, and cut out the eye holes with a scissors.

Cut the cardboard tube so that it is 20 inches (51 centimeters) long. Glue the tube along the center of the mask, between the eye holes, to make the crest. Use some masking tape to hold it in place while the glue is drying.

16

3 Cut the blower off the party horn. Mark where your chin rests in the mask and then cut a small hole through the mask and one side of the tube at that mark. Slide the end of the horn into the hole at an angle so that it tips up easily to reach your mouth when you are wearing the mask.

5 This mask looks wonderful with a layer of tissue-paper skin over it. This is messy so be sure to put down newspaper to work on. Mix 1 cup (250 milliliters) of glue with ¼ cup (60 milliliters) of water in a bowl. Dip a piece of tissue large enough to cover the mask into the glue mixture. Lay the tissue paper on top of the mask, shaping it over the tube. Fold the edges behind the front of the mask. Do not worry about holes if there are any. Just slide the tissue paper together or patch the holes with more pieces of tissue. The skin will look rough and irregular when it dries. Poke holes in the tissue over the eyes. Let the mask dry completely on Styrofoam trays. Be sure to put newspaper underneath them.

4 Punch a hole on each edge of the mask, at the same height as the eyes. Tie an 8-inch (20-centimeter) piece of string through each hole so that you can tie the mask on.

Put on your Parasaurolophus mask and blow the horn to make a noise that will come through the crest.

Baryonyx Flip Game

Here is what you need:

two cardboard paper-towel tubes
cereal-box cardboard
cardboard egg carton
wooden ice-cream spoon
yarn
aluminum foil
black permanent marker
pinking shears
hole punch
white glue

scissors
masking tape
white and red poster paint
   and other colors of your
   choice
paint brush
cotton swab
newspaper to work on
Styrofoam tray to dry
   your project on

The most remarkable thing about the Baryonyx is its enormous claws. Many scientists think that the dinosaur used these hooked claws to hunt fish.

Here is what you do:

With the pinking shears, cut a triangle-shaped wedge, 3 inches (7.6 centimeters) long, out of each side of one end of a tube. This will be the dinosaur's mouth, full of sharp teeth.

Cut a slit 6 inches (15 centimeters) long in the other tube. Wrap the two edges of the cut tube around each other to form a cone. Hold the cone shape in place with masking tape. Cut a slit 4 inches (10 centimeters) long in the other end of the tube. Rub glue around the outside of the cut tube and slide it into the first tube, with the cone end out, to form the tail of the dinosaur.

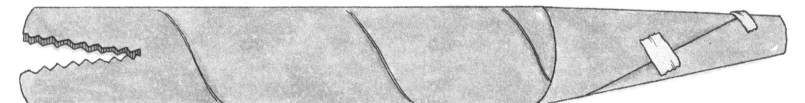

18

Cut two legs and two arms from cardboard. Cut two points in each of the arms to make two small claws. Glue the arms and legs on the sides of the dinosaur.

Cut three egg cups from the egg carton and glue them on the back of the dinosaur. Let the glue dry.

Paint the inside of the mouth of the dinosaur red. Paint the body of the dinosaur with the colors of your choice. Let the paint dry.

To make the large claws, cut the two ends off the cotton swab. Glue one end to each arm of the dinosaur. Let the glue dry.

7. With aluminum foil, shape a large claw around the cotton swab on each of the front feet of the dinosaur.

8. Paint the points made by the pinking shears around the mouth of the dinosaur white to look like teeth.

9. Cut a piece of yarn 20 inches (51 centimeters) long. Tie one end of the yarn around the ice-cream spoon. Wrap the spoon and the tied end of the yarn with aluminum foil to make a small fish. Leave the rest of the yarn free. Use markers to draw an eye on each side of the large end of the spoon and decorate the body of the fish.

10. Punch a hole in the bottom lip of the dinosaur. Tie the other end of the yarn with the fish on it through the hole.

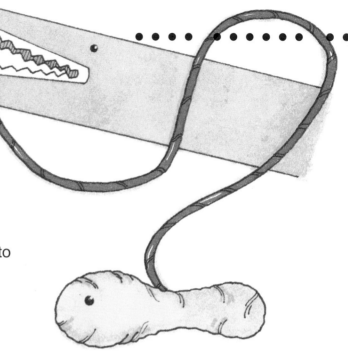

Fish scales were found near the stomach area of the first Baryonyx fossil, so scientists believe the dinosaur may have used its huge claws to catch fish to eat. Can you feed your Baryonyx by flipping the fish into its mouth?

Dinosaur Window Scenes

Here is what you need:

permanent markers in several colors
plastic wrap
dinosaur books or coloring books

Here is what you do:

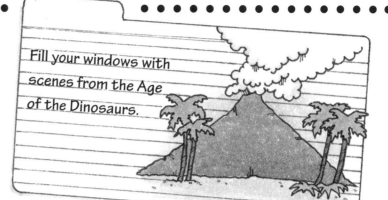

Fill your windows with scenes from the Age of the Dinosaurs.

1) Tear off a large square of plastic wrap. Choose a simple drawing of a dinosaur from a book or coloring book. Place the plastic wrap over the drawing and trace the dinosaur. Find pictures of prehistoric plants, too, and add them to the scene.

2) Color the prehistoric scene with permanent markers.

3) The plastic wrap will stick to the window. It will look as if the scene is drawn directly on the glass.

You can also make your own drawings on the plastic wrap rather than tracing a picture.

21

Tyrannosaurus Rex Treasure Keeper

Here is what you need:

two plastic gallon-size milk jugs
spray paint in the color of your choice
jumbo white rickrack
masking tape
two paper fasteners
hole punch
scissors
blue glue gel
black marker

Tyrannosaurus Rex was the largest of the meat-eating dinosaurs. Some scientists believe this dinosaur was a quick and fearsome hunter. Others think Tyrannosaurus was a lazy dinosaur who liked an easy meal left by other meat eaters.

Here is what you do:

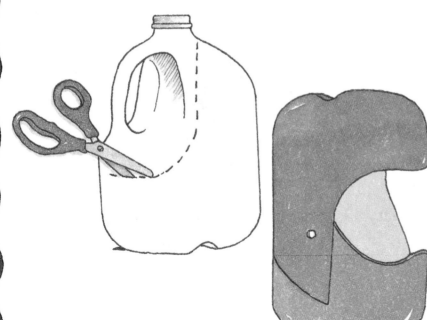

Cut around the spout and handle portion of both jugs to remove them. Turn one jug upside-down and slide it over the other jug to form a container with an opening where the handles were cut out. The opening will be the mouth of the dinosaur. Punch a hole through both containers on each side of the mouth. Later, you will hold the two containers together by putting a paper fastener through each of the holes.

Spray both containers with the paint color of your choice. Before you do this, ask a grownup at your house for permission. It's best to do this outdoors, and you may need to have an adult do it for you. Let the containers dry.

3 Put a strip of masking tape along the inside edge of the mouth opening of each container. This will help the rickrack teeth stick to the plastic. Insert a paper fastener in each of the two holes to hold the containers together. Glue the rickrack along the inside edge of the top and the bottom of the mouth.

4 Cut eyes from masking tape and stick them on each side of the head above the mouth. Draw a pupil in the middle of each eye with the black marker.

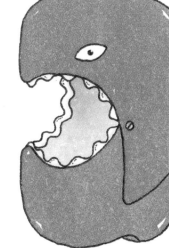

Put Tyrannosaurus Rex on your dresser to keep important stuff in.

Dimetrodon Magnet

Here is what you need:

two wooden ice-cream spoons
craft stick
disposable aluminum pie pan
masking tape
scissors
paintbrush and poster paint in color of your choice
black permanent marker
white glue
piece of sticky-backed magnet
Styrofoam tray to work on

The Dimetrodon was an early reptile that predated the first dinosaurs. This creature is distinguished by a large sail-shaped curve on its back.

Here is what you do:

The two ice-cream spoons will form the body of the Dimetrodon. The large ends of the spoons should be the dinosaur's head. To make the Dimetrodon's legs, cut a piece about 1 inch (2.5 centimeters) long from each end of the craft stick. Glue the stick legs, rounded ends down, to one of the spoons. Let the glue dry.

Paint both halves of the body, including the legs, and let them dry.

3 Draw a face and claws on the reptile with the black marker.

4 Cut a semicircle 2 inches (5 centimeters) wide from the ripply edge of the pie tin to make the sail-shaped curve. Cover both sides of the straight edge of the sail with masking tape and then cover the tape with glue. (Glue won't stick to aluminum, but it will stick to masking tape.) Glue the sail to the back of one of the painted spoons. Then glue on the second wooden spoon to form the other half of the body. Let the glue dry.

5 Press a piece of sticky-backed magnet to the back of the Dimetrodon.

Stick this prehistoric favorite on your refrigerator for everyone to admire.

Gliding Archaeopteryx

Here is what you need:

toy airplane glider
12-inch (30-centimeter) pipe cleaner
craft feathers in colors of your choice
masking tape
white glue
scissors
black marker

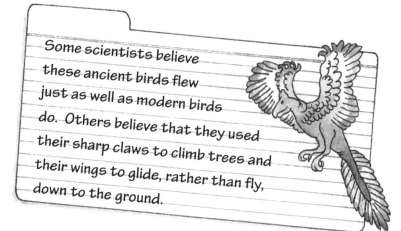

Some scientists believe these ancient birds flew just as well as modern birds do. Others believe that they used their sharp claws to climb trees and their wings to glide, rather than fly, down to the ground.

Here is what you do:

1. If the glider you are using is made of Styrofoam rather than cardboard or balsa wood, cover the top and sides with strips of masking tape to help the feathers stick.

2. Cut a 6-inch (15-centimeter) piece of pipe cleaner. Wrap it around the center of the glider behind the wings and let the two ends hang down to form the legs of the bird. Wrap a smaller piece of pipe cleaner around the bottom of each leg to form claws.

Glue feathers all over the bird. Be careful not to make the bird too heavy or it won't glide. Use only a thin coating of glue and just enough feathers to cover the glider.

Cut two eyes from masking tape and stick one on each side of the front of the glider. Draw pupils on each eye with black marker.

Put some plastic or paper insects on the ground for your bird's dinner and see if you can get the Archaeopteryx to land on top of one.

Plesiosaur Window Decoration

Here is what you need:

plastic egg left over from Easter
aluminum foil
colorful markers
masking tape
black and blue permanent markers
quart-size zip-to-close bag
hole punch
yarn
scissors

The Plesiosaurs were among the many strange-looking reptiles that filled the seas during the Age of the Dinosaurs.

Here is what you do:

Tear off about 7 inches (18 centimeters) of aluminum foil. Wrap the foil around the plastic egg, leaving about 2 inches (5 centimeters) of foil at one end of the egg to form the tail and the rest of the foil at the other end to form a long neck.

Squeeze the foil for the neck and the tail into tight, thin strips. Point the tail slightly downward. Point the neck upward and tip the end forward to shape a head. Squeeze the front of the head into a point.

With the black marker, draw eyes on the head and flipper-like arms and legs on each side of the egg body.

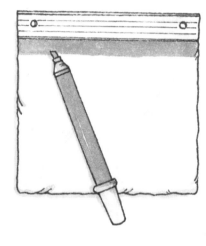

To make an environment for the Plesiosaur to live in, color the back of the zip-to-close bag with the blue marker to make it look like water. Punch a hole on each side of the top of the bag and tie on a yarn hanger.

Draw some tiny fish on masking tape. Color the fish and cut them out. Stick the fish in the bag for the Plesiosaur to eat for dinner.

Put the Plesiosaur in the bag and hang it in a sunny window.

Dinosaur Feet

Here is what you need:

four large brown grocery bags
newspaper for stuffing
four large white Styrofoam trays
masking tape
white glue
scissors

Get together with your friends to make these giant dinosaur feet.

Here is what you do:

1 Stuff a grocery bag loosely with crumpled newspaper. Slide a second bag over the opening of the stuffed bag. Pull the top bag all the way down over the stuffed one.

2 About 3 inches (7.6 centimeters) up from the bottom of the top bag, cut a hole 4 inches (10 centimeters) wide. Fold masking tape around the cut edge of the opening. This will help to keep the hole from tearing while you're wearing the foot.

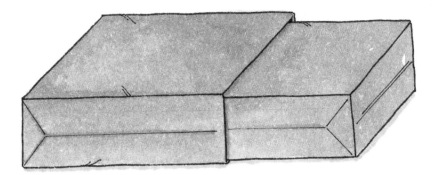

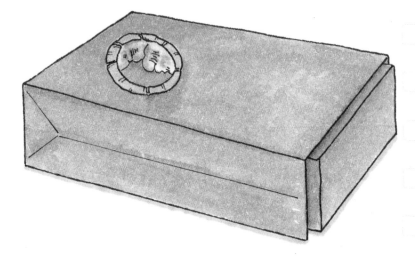

Out of Styrofoam, cut four triangle-shaped claws with sides 3 inches (7.6 centimeters) long. Put masking tape across the front and back of one side of each triangle. The tape will help the glue stick to the claws. Rub glue on the tape and slip the claws into the opening between the top bag and the stuffed bag. Make the second foot the same way.

To wear the dinosaur feet, place your feet in the holes and snuggle them down into the crumpled newspaper. Practice stomping around like a dinosaur. (Please be careful when wearing your dinosaur feet. Dinosaurs should not climb stairs.)

Books About Dinosaurs

Aliki. *Digging Up Dinosaurs*. New York: Crowell, 1981.

Aliki. *My Visit to the Dinosaurs*. New York: Crowell, 1969.

Caket, Colin. *Model a Monster: Making Dinosaurs from Everyday Materials*. Poole: Blandford, 1986.

Clark, Neil. *A Look Inside Dinosaurs*. Pleasantville, NY: Reader's Digest Association, 1995.

Dixon, Dougal. *Dougal Dixon's Dinosaurs*. Honesdale, PA: Boyds Mills Press, 1993.

Glut, Donald F. *Discover Dinosaurs*. Lincolnwood, IL: Publications International, 1993.

Ipcar, Dahlov Zorach. *The Wonderful Egg*. Garden City, NY: Doubleday, 1958.

Jaber, William. *Whatever Happened to the Dinosaurs*. New York: J. Messner, 1978.

Johnson, Kirk R. *Prehistoric Journey: A History of Life on Earth*. Denver: Denver Museum of Natural History; Boulder: Roberts Rinehart, 1995.

Martin, Alice Fitch. *Dinosaurs: A Golden Exploring Earth Book*. Racine, WI: Golden Press, 1973.

McGowen, Tom. *Album of Dinosaurs*. Chicago: Rand McNally, 1972.

Packard, Mary. *The Dinosaurs*. New York: Little Simon, 1981.

Parker, Steve. *Inside Dinosaurs and Other Prehistoric Creatures*. New York: Delacorte Press, 1994.

Petty, Kate. *Dinosaurs*. New York: Gloucester Press, 1988.

Pringle, Laurence P. *Dinosaurs and People: Fossils, Facts, and Fantasies*. New York: Harcourt Brace Jovanovich, 1978.

Rao, Anthony. *The Dinosaur Coloring Book*. New York: Dover Publications, 1980.

Senior, Kathryn. *The X-Ray Picture Book of Dinosaurs and Other Prehistoric Creatures*. New York: Franklin Watts, 1994.

Unwin, David. *The New Book of Dinosaurs*. Brookfield, CT: Copper Beech, 1997.

Oceans

The oceans have been called by many, the last frontier. Amazing plant and animal life are still being discovered and studied. Most of the vast ocean floor has never even been viewed by people.

If you find the mysterious ocean world fascinating, or if you're a kid who likes to poke around the beach, try some of the projects in this section. The Water-Spouting Whale or the Fish Swimming Through Seaweed Puppet would make nice models for a science presentation. Or, you may want to add a little ocean atmosphere at home. The Soft Sculpture Snail would make a great decorative pillow, and the Angelfish Wall Hanging would add some pizzaz to your décor—and use up a lot of your dad's old neckties at the same time!

The projects included in this section are based on some of the better-known inhabitants of the deep. If you really want to meet some fascinating creatures, check out some of the books on ocean life listed on page 56.

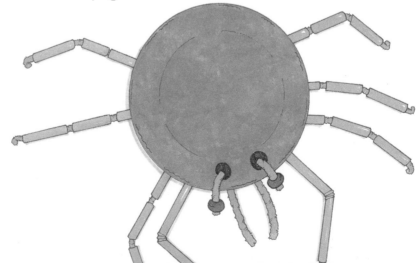

Ocean in a Bag

Here is what you need:

two sturdy zip-to-close bags of the same size
Styrofoam trays in several different colors
white or pastel-colored plastic beads from old jewelry
blue hair gel
small seashells
clear packing tape

Here is what you do:

Fill one of the bags with blue hair gel so that, when the bag is closed and flattened out, the gel is about ¼ to ½ inch (about 1 cm) thick all over the inside surface of the bag.

Cut 1- to 2-inch (2.5 to 5 cm) -long fish from several different colored Styrofoam trays. (If you can't find colored trays, you can color white ones. Just be sure to use permanent markers.) Put them in the bag. Toss in a few seashells and add some plastic beads for bubbles.

More than two-thirds of the world's surface is covered by water.

BLUE Hair GEL

3 Squeeze as much air as possible out of the partially closed bag, then seal the bag. Place the bag, sealed end first, inside the other bag. Zip the second bag closed. Cover the closed edge of the bag with clear tape.

Run your hands over the surface of the bag to make the fish move around in the gel "water." But be careful—there is something so soothing about playing with this project that it is hard to put down!

Think about what else you might add to your ocean, such as glitter or different ocean animals.

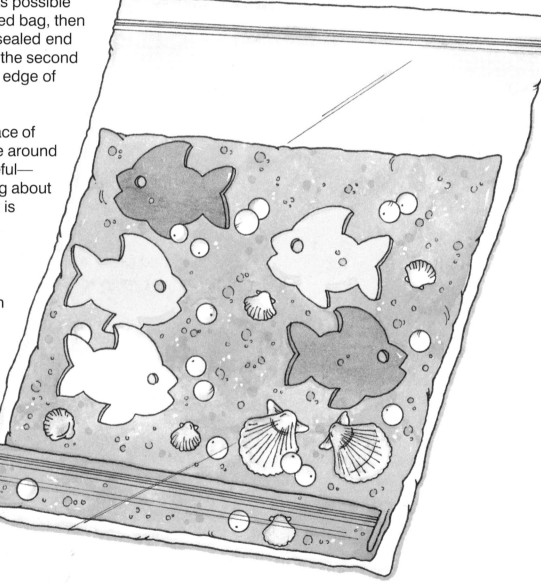

Here is what you need:

a pair of light-colored adult-size knit gloves
five brightly colored pom-poms
felt scraps
brown or very dark green tissue paper
string
white paper scrap
sharp black marker
hole punch
scissors
white glue
brown poster paint and a paintbrush
Styrofoam tray for drying

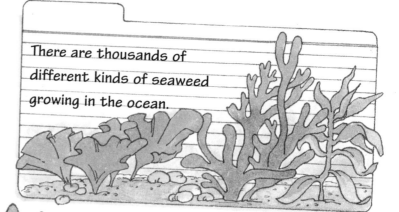

There are thousands of different kinds of seaweed growing in the ocean.

Here is what you do:

Paint one of the gloves brown. Let the paint dry.

Cut long leaves of seaweed from the tissue paper, and glue them up and down both sides of the painted glove.

Turn the five pom-poms into little fish. Cut tails and fins from felt scraps and glue them in place. Punch an eye for each fish from white paper. Draw a pupil on each eye.

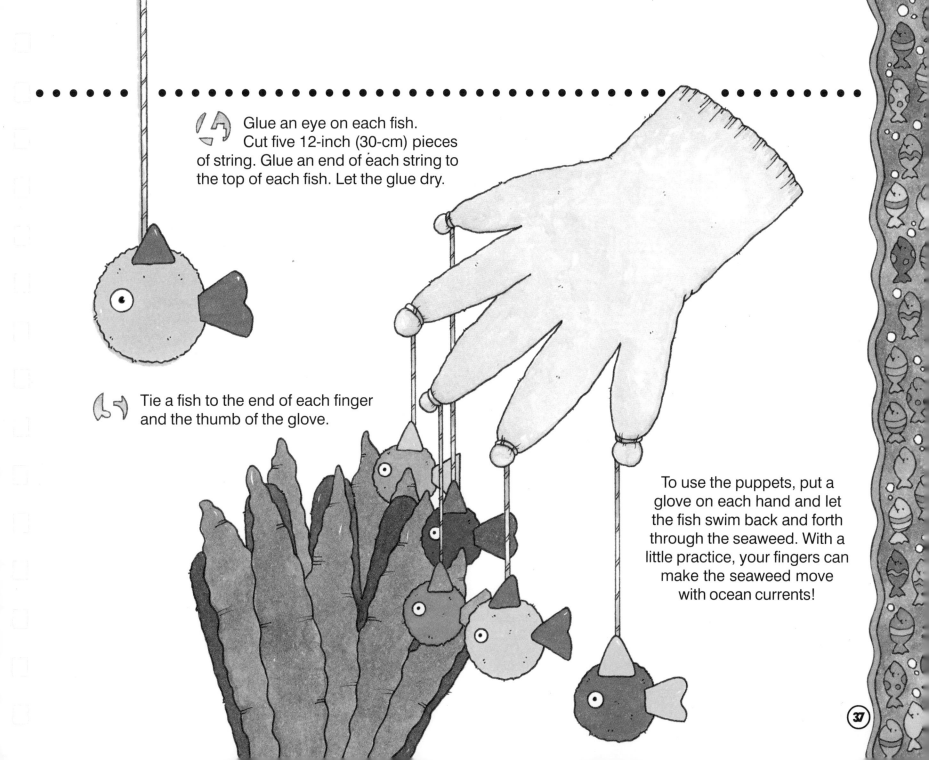

Glue an eye on each fish. Cut five 12-inch (30-cm) pieces of string. Glue an end of each string to the top of each fish. Let the glue dry.

Tie a fish to the end of each finger and the thumb of the glove.

To use the puppets, put a glove on each hand and let the fish swim back and forth through the seaweed. With a little practice, your fingers can make the seaweed move with ocean currents!

Clam Puppet

Here is what you need:

two 9-inch (23-cm) paper plates
old white sock
gray poster paint and a paintbrush
stapler and staples
two large wiggle eyes
scissors
Styrofoam tray for drying

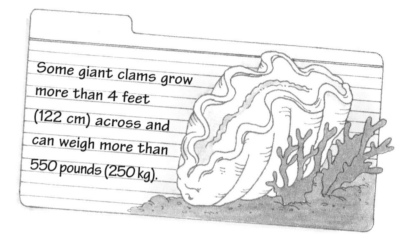

Some giant clams grow more than 4 feet (122 cm) across and can weigh more than 550 pounds (250 kg).

Here is what you do:

Fold a paper plate in half and staple it to keep it folded. Repeat with the second plate.

Place the two folded plates on top of each other to form the top and bottom of a clam-shell. Use the scissors to round off each of the corners of the flat sides of the two plates to make them look more like a shell. Staple the two plates together on each side of the back of the shell.

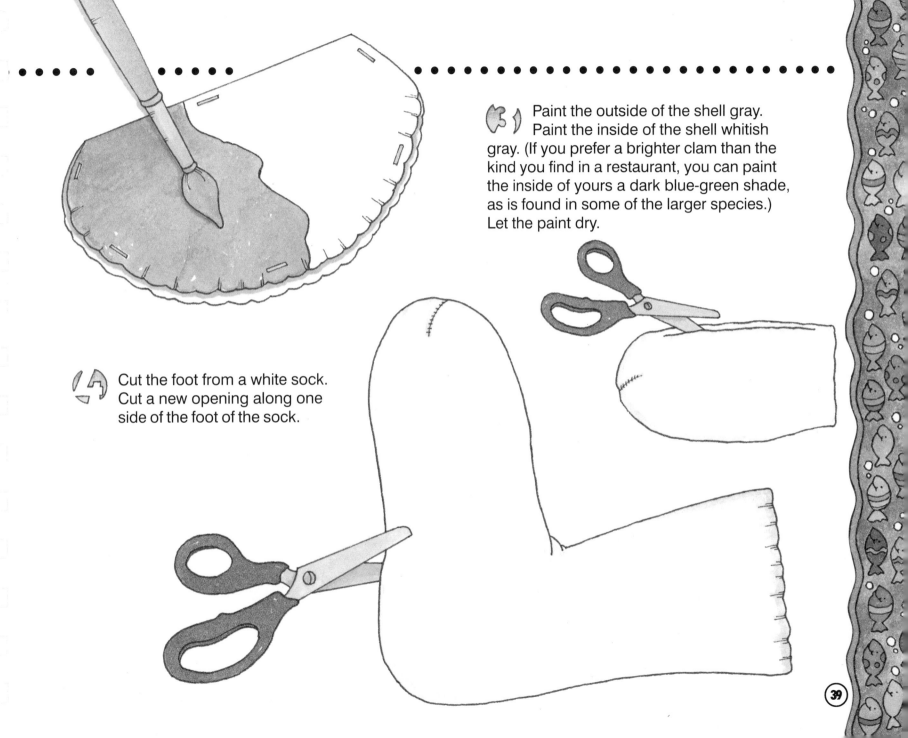

Paint the outside of the shell gray. Paint the inside of the shell whitish gray. (If you prefer a brighter clam than the kind you find in a restaurant, you can paint the inside of yours a dark blue-green shade, as is found in some of the larger species.) Let the paint dry.

Cut the foot from a white sock. Cut a new opening along one side of the foot of the sock.

To make the clam inside the shell, staple the top of the cut opening of the sock inside the back part of the top of the shell and staple the bottom cut opening of the sock to the bottom of the shell. Before putting in the final staple, pull any excess sock material together and staple it neatly.

Glue two large wiggle eyes on the clam or make your own eyes from felt or cut paper.

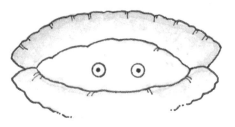

To open and shut the clam, put your thumb on the bottom of the shell and your pinkie on top. Your other fingers go inside the clam so you can make it wiggle when the shell opens.

Pile of Sea Urchins

Here is what you need:

three 2-inch (5-cm) Styrofoam balls
toothpicks
poster paints in three bright colors and a paintbrush
white glue
clear plastic glitter, or salt
margarine tubs and plastic spoons for mixing
Styrofoam tray for drying
newspaper to work on

Here is what you do:

Cover all three Styrofoam balls with toothpicks to make spines on each sea urchin. You can paint your sea urchins fanciful colors, or you can look for pictures of real sea urchins and copy those colors. Mix a small amount of white glue into each color of paint you use. Paint each sea urchin a different color, then immediately sprinkle the wet paint with glitter or salt.

When the sea urchins are dry, press them gently together until the toothpicks of one connect with the body of another. A pile of sea urchins makes a pretty display.

The sea urchin comes in a variety of shapes and sizes, but always with spines.

41

Soft Sculpture Snail

Here is what you need:

pair of old pantyhose
fiberfill
two safety pins
two large wiggle eyes
pipe cleaner
white glue
scissors
poster paint and a paintbrush
Styrofoam tray to work on

Fossil records show that snails have lived in the oceans for more than 500 million years.

Here is what you do:

Cut one leg off the pantyhose. Stuff the leg evenly with fiberfill to about 4 inches (10 cm) from the opening. Hold the edges of the stuffed leg of the pantyhose together and tuck the seam down between the stuffing and the stocking on one side.

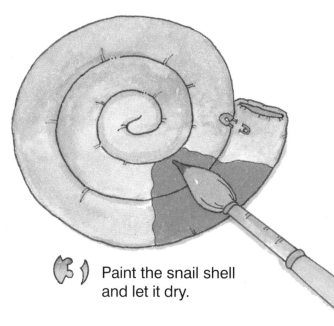

Starting at the foot, roll the stuffed leg to make a spiraled snail shell. Use the two safety pins to hold the rolled stocking in place by pinning it to itself on each side of the opening. Rub glue between the folds of the wrapped stocking leg to help hold it in place.

Paint the snail shell and let it dry.

To make the snail head, cut the foot from the second stocking. Stuff half of the foot with fiberfill. Push the unstuffed end of the foot down into the opening of the shell, between the two safety pins, so that the stuffed end sticks out like a head peeking out of a shell. Rub glue around the inner opening of the shell to hold the head in place.

Cut a 6-inch (15-cm) piece of pipe cleaner. Poke one end through one side of the top of the snail head and out the other side to make antennae for the snail. Curl the end of each antenna into a tiny knob.

Glue two wiggle eyes on the front of the snail head.

Maybe you should make a friend for your snail.

Sea Star

Here is what you need:

light cardboard
pencil
paper fastener
yellow poster paint and paintbrush
white glue
sand
scissors
margarine tub and plastic spoon for mixing
newspaper to work on

If a sea star is unfortunate enough to lose one of its arms, it is able to grow a new one!

Here is what you do:

Draw the shape of a sea star on cardboard. Cut the shape out.

Cut one arm off the sea star. Use it as a pattern to draw a new arm with extra cardboard on it so that it can be attached to the back of the sea star. Cut out the arm.

3) Attach the new arm to the sea star with a paper fastener. The arm should be able to swing behind the sea star so that it cannot be seen, then swing back out to allow the sea star to "grow" a new arm. If the attached arm shows when swung behind the sea star, trim the edges slightly until it cannot be seen.

4) Mix a small amount of white glue with some yellow paint. Paint the sea star and immediately sprinkle it with the sand to give it a rough texture. Let the paint dry completely.

This sea star can lose an arm and grow it back just like a real one. But make sure to keep it away from the shark on page 50!

45

Jellyfish Windsock

Here is what you need:

two clear kitchen trash bags
cellophane tape
string
clear Con-tac paper
black marker
sequins
tissue paper in many different colors
stapler and staples
scissors

The jellyfish moves through the water trailing its poisonous tentacles along to capture and eat fish and other sea creatures. The tentacles of some jellyfish can be up to 160 feet (36.5 meters) long!

Here is what you do:

Crumple one of the trash bags into a ball and stuff it into the corner of the other bag. The ball will be the head of the jellyfish. Tape around the bottom of the ball to form a neck.

Cut part of the trash bag hanging down from the head into long strips to make the tentacles.

Push a string through the neck of the jellyfish and tie the two ends together to make a hanger for the windsock.

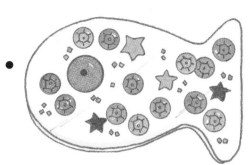

For each fish you make you will need to cut two identical fish shapes from a piece of clear Con-tac paper. Peel the protective backing off one shape and decorate the sticky side with bits of colored tissue paper and sequins. Cut out an eye from tissue and draw a pupil in the center. Stick the eye at the head end of the fish. Cover the fish with the other piece of Contac paper so that the sequins and tissue paper are layered between the two pieces. Make at least three colorful fish.

Staple each fish to a jellyfish tentacle.

Find a breezy place to hang the jellyfish windsock.

Angelfish Wall Hanging

Here is what you need:

five or six old neckties
corrugated cardboard
bubble wrap with large bubbles
scrap of black paper
blue poster paint and paintbrush
scissors
hole punch
piece of yarn
white glue

Some species of angelfish are believed to be among the few animals that mate for life.

Here is what you do:

Cut a 15-inch (38-cm) circle from the cardboard.

Paint the cardboard circle blue and let it dry.

To make each fish, cut a 6-inch (15-cm) -long piece from the wide end of a necktie. Round off the cut end of the tie to form the back of the fish. Cut a 2½-inch (6.3-cm) piece from the small end of the same tie or a different one for the tail of the fish. Cut a top and bottom fin on the fold of the tie scraps.

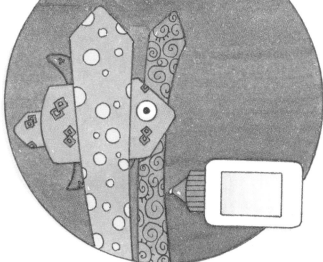

4 Cut four 10- to 12-inch (25- to 30-cm) pieces of seaweed from the narrow ends of the neckties. If the piece is not an end cut, you will need to cut the piece into a point at one end.

5 Arrange the seaweed pieces so that they come up from the bottom of the circle. Tuck the angelfish bodies between and behind the seaweed to look like they are swimming through it. Add the tails and fins. When you have an arrangement you like, glue everything in place.

6 Cut a large bubble out of the bubble wrap for each fish. Cut a pupil from the black paper for each eye. Cut a tiny slit in the back of each bubble and slip a pupil into each eye. Glue an eye on each fish.

7 Punch a hole in the top of the cardboard. String a piece of yarn through the hole and tie the two ends together to make a hanger.

Hang up these beautiful and unusual fish for all to admire.

Scary Shark Puppet

Here is what you need:

two 42-ounce (1,193-gram) oatmeal boxes
adult-size black or dark-gray sock
black construction paper
two cotton balls
scissors
white glue
masking tape

Here is what you do:

1. Cut down the side of one of the oatmeal boxes. Cut the rim off the top of the box. Cut out the bottom of the box.

2. Carefully peel the printed outer layer off the upper portion of the box to expose the gray cardboard underlayer.

3. Cut 1-inch (2.5-cm) -long pointed teeth all the way around the peeled rim of the box. If you want the teeth to look whiter than the color of the cardboard, you will need to paint them.

Because a shark has no swim bladder, it must swim constantly or it will sink deep into the ocean and die.

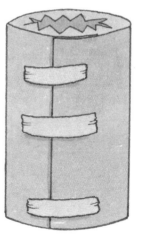

4. Wrap the cut box around itself until the mouth opening is about 4 inches (10 cm) across. Wrap the outside of the box with strips of masking tape to hold the rolled cardboard in place.

Cut out the bottom of the second oatmeal box.

Cut the toe off the sock so that it is open at both ends. Slide the sock over the second box to cover it with the cuff at the rimmed top of the box. The sock should be pulled over the box so that the cuff forms a closed mouth for the shark and the foot end of the sock closes over the tail end of the shark.

Cut two side fins from the black paper and glue them in place by making a fold along the fin to glue to the shark. Cut two identical top fins from the black paper. Glue the two pieces together, first spreading the two sides out at the bottom to form a fold to glue onto the top of the shark.

Glue two cotton balls on the cuffed end to make eyes. Cut pupils from the black paper and glue them in place.

To use the shark puppet, slide the teeth into the back of the shark so that they are hidden inside the box body. By pushing on the inner box you will cause the teeth to emerge from the mouth of the shark with a surprising show of ferocity. Yikes!

Water-spouting Whale

Here is what you need:

gallon-size plastic milk jug
14½-ounce (435-ml) dish detergent bottle
aluminum foil
black permanent marker
scissors
masking tape

Here is what you do:

When a whale comes to the surface, it sprays out a mist of air and water. If a whale does not surface at regular intervals to breathe, it will drown.

1. Cut around the entire handle and neck portion of the bottle to remove the top section.

2. Turn the remaining bottle on its side so that one of the corners is the bottom of the whale body. Cut a small hole in the center of the top corner of the jug for the spout. The detergent bottle should be able to fit inside the whale body with the top of the bottle up through the cut hole.

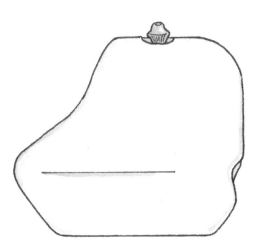

3) Cover the entire milk jug with aluminum foil. Poke through the foil to open up the blowhole. Shape a tail for the whale from foil and tape it to the open end of the bottle down from the spout.

4) Use the permanent marker to give the whale a face.

To use the spouting whale, fill the detergent bottle to the top with water. Replace the cap, making sure the spout on top of the cap is pulled to the open position. Slip the bottle back inside the whale with the spout up through the cut hole. Take the whale outside or into the bathtub. When you squeeze the bottle, the spray can't be seen for miles, but it shoots high enough to get the area very wet!

Leaping Dolphin Puppet

Here is what you need:

16-ounce (473-ml) plastic soda bottle
adult-size dark-gray sock
adult-size white sock with very stretchy cuff
blue poster paint and a paintbrush
square tissue box
black permanent marker
fiberfill
white glue
scissors

The jaw line of the bottlenose dolphin makes it look as though it is always smiling!

Here is what you do:

Cut off the base of the bottle.

Put the bottle inside the gray sock, spout first, so that the open end of the bottle is at the open end of the sock.

The seam on top of the toe of the sock forms a mouth for the dolphin. Use the black marker to draw eyes.

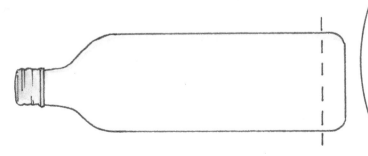

4. Rub white glue on the stomach portion of the dolphin. Cover the glue with fiberfill to make the white underbelly.

5. Cut the bottom out of the tissue box.

6. Cut the stretchy cuff from the white sock. Use the cuff to cover the tissue box.

7. Paint the sock-covered box blue for water.

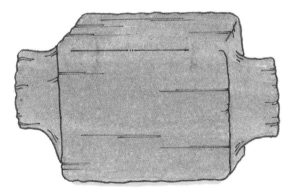

Push the nose end of the dolphin puppet up through the bottom of the box and through the opening at the top. To move the puppet, slip your hand up through the bottom of the box and inside the dolphin.

Books About Oceans

Baker, Lucy. *Life in the Oceans.* New York: Franklin Watts, 1990.

Bramwell, Martyn. *The Oceans.* New York: Franklin Watts, 1987.

Carter, Katherine Jones. *Oceans.* Chicago: Childrens Press, 1982.

Cole, Joanna. *The Magic School Bus on the Ocean Floor.* New York: Scholastic, 1992.

Cook, Jan Leslie. *The Mysterious Undersea World.* Washington, D.C.: National Geographic Society, 1980.

Craig, Janet. *What's Under the Ocean?* Mahwah, NJ: Troll, 1982.

Crema, Laura. *Look Inside the Ocean.* New York: Grosset & Dunlap, 1993.

Ganeri, Anita. *The Oceans Atlas.* London; New York: Dorling Kindersley, 1994.

Hoff, Mary King. *Our Endangered Planet.* Minneapolis: Lerner Publications, 1991.

Jennings, Terry. *Oceans and Seas.* Danbury, CT: Grolier Education Corporation, 1992.

Knight, David C. *Let's Find Out About the Ocean.* New York: Franklin Watts, 1970.

Lambert, David. *Seas and Oceans.* Morristown, NJ: Silver Burdett Press, 1988.

MacQuitty, Miranda. *Ocean.* New York: Knopf, 1995.

Morris, Neil. *Oceans.* New York: Crabtree Publishing Co.,1996.

Mudd-Ruth, Maria. *The Ultimate Ocean Book.* New York: Artists & Writers Guild Books/Golden Books/ Western Publishing, 1995.

O'Mara, Anna. *Oceans.* Mankato, MN: Bridgestone Books, 1996.

Sayre, April. *Ocean.* New York: Twenty-First Century Books, 1996.

Talbot, Frank (Editor). *Under the Sea.* Alexandria, VA: Time-Life Books, 1995.

Yardley, Thompson. *Make a Splash.* Brookfield, CT: Millbrook Press, 1992.

Polar Life

This section tells how to make some of the animals that live in the very coldest places on our earth—the polar regions. The temperature in these regions rarely goes above freezing, so the land and the surrounding seas are frozen for much of the year.

The Arctic is made up of the Arctic Ocean and the land around it, which is called the tundra. Many animals spend their summer in the Arctic, and others stay there year-round.

The Antarctic consists of the continent of Antarctica, the Southern Ocean surrounding it, and the islands in the Southern Ocean. Antarctica is so cold that only a few plants and some insects manage to survive there. However, the waters surrounding Antarctica support a variety of life-forms.

For a dramatic science project presentation of tundra life, make the Caribou Marionette or the Changing-Coat Hare. The Penguin Pin would look great on a winter coat, and the Snarling Wolf Face is an original Halloween idea. Whatever projects you choose, I hope they will make you want to read some of the books listed on page 80 to find out more about the way these creatures live and survive in the frozen world of the North and South Poles.

Penguin Pin

Here is what you need:

three wooden ice-cream spoons
black poster paint and a paintbrush
white glue
fiberfill
scrap of orange felt
two wiggle eyes
masking tape
pin backing or safety pin
Styrofoam tray for drying

Penguins are birds that cannot fly in the air, but they "fly" underwater, using the same muscles other birds use to fly in the air.

Here is what you do:

Paint one side and the edge of two of the ice-cream spoons black. Put them on the Styrofoam tray to dry.

Use glue to cover one side of the third spoon with a thin layer of fiberfill.

3) Glue the handle ends of the two black spoons together so that the bowl ends flare out on each side to make wings. Glue the fiberfill-covered spoon behind and between the wings so that the white fiberfill forms the tummy of the penguin.

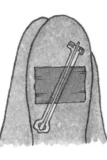

4) Cut a triangle-shaped beak from the orange felt scrap. Glue the two wiggle eyes and the beak on the black overlapped handles above the white tummy.

5) Glue the pin backing or safety pin to the back of the penguin. Use a piece of masking tape to hold the pin in place while the glue is drying.

This penguin also makes a very nice refrigerator magnet. Just use a piece of sticky-back magnet instead of the pin.

Fuzzy Polar Bear

Here is what you need:

four clamp clothespins
two wooden tongue depressors
fiberfill
white felt scrap
three tiny black beads or peppercorns
small white pom-pom
scissors
white glue
Styrofoam tray for drying

The world's largest bear, the polar bear, lives in the Arctic.

Here is what you do:

Clamp a clothespin to one end of one of the tongue depressors. Clamp a second clothespin about 1 inch (2.5 cm) from the other end of the stick. Use glue to hold the clothespins in place. Do the same thing with the second tongue depressor. The sticks will form the two sides of the body of the bear, and the clothespins will form the legs, with the head of the bear formed by the inch of stick left at one end.

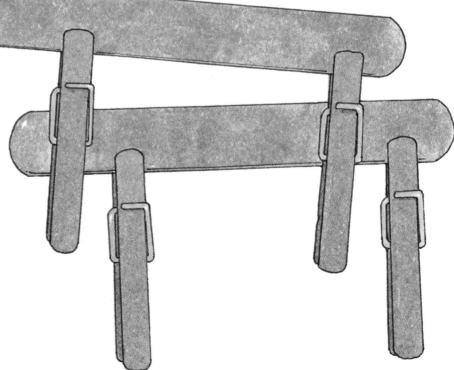

Cover each set of clothespin legs and stick body with glue, then wrap them with fiberfill. Glue the two sides of the body together and let the project dry on the Styrofoam tray.

Cut two ears for the bear from the white felt scrap. Glue the ears to the top of the head. Glue the white pom-pom on the front of the head to form a muzzle. Glue a black bead on the end of the muzzle for a nose. Glue the other two beads above the muzzle to make eyes.

A newborn polar bear cub is so tiny, it can actually hide between its mother's toes—but it doesn't stay tiny for long.

Snarling Wolf Face

Here is what you need:

two 9-inch (23-cm) paper plates
white Styrofoam cup
two paper fasteners
small red sock
white and black construction-paper scraps
fiberfill
gray poster paint and a paintbrush
scissors
white glue
masking tape
stapler

Arctic wolves live and hunt together in groups called packs.

Here is what you do:

1. Cut the Styrofoam cup in half from top to bottom. Cut pointy teeth along the cut edges of both halves of the cup.

2. Overlap the rim of the two halves of the cup and hold them together with a paper fastener on each side. The two halves of the cup should now form a mouth with teeth that opens and shuts.

3. Hold the two plates together and, toward one edge, cut a hole in them large enough to slip the mouth through, but not large enough for the rim of the cup to go through. Put the mouth through from the eating side of one plate so that it comes out from the bottom of the plate. Use masking tape to tape the mouth to the plate. Glue the second plate over the first plate.

62

4. Cover the Styrofoam mouth with strips of masking tape to create a better gluing surface. Glue fiberfill all over the face and mouth of the wolf.

5. Cut the foot of the red sock in half. Slip the toe half into the mouth of the wolf from the back of the head to make a tongue. Staple the end of the sock tongue to the bottom of the plate to hold it in place.

6. Cut two ears from the white paper. Glue them to the top of the wolf's head.

7. Cut two eyes from black paper and glue them above the mouth.

8. Dab the ears and fiberfill with gray paint.

9. Glue the black pom-pom on the cup mouth to make a nose.

To use your plate wolf face, slip the fingers of one hand into the tongue to wiggle it as you open and shut the mouth with your other hand.

Changing Coat Hare

Here is what you need:

9-inch (23-cm) paper plates
fiberfill
white, black, and brown construction paper
two clamp clothespins
brown poster paint and a paintbrush
black marker
white glue
scissors
newspaper to work on

The snowshoe hare changes from a white winter coat that hides it in the snow to a brown coat that matches the background of the short Arctic summer.

Here is what you do:

Paint one side of the plate brown. Cover the other side of the plate with fiberfill.

To make the winter hare, fold the plate in half with the white fiberfill on the outside. Use one of the clothespins to hold the plate edges together. Cut two eyes from the black paper and glue them on each side of one end of the plate.

3 Position the holding clothespin just behind and above the eyes for ears. Cut two ears from the white paper. Color the tip of each ear black. Glue an ear over each side of the clothespin.

4 To make the summer hare, remove the white ears and fold the plate so that the brown side is on the outside. Hold the fold with the second clothespin. Cut two eyes from black paper and glue them in place. Position the clothespin above and behind the eyes for the ears. Cut two ears from brown paper. Color the tip of each ear black. Glue an ear on each side of the clothespin.

To change the coat of your snowshoe hare, just fold the plate with the desired coat on the outside and hold the fold in place with the correct color ears.

Caribou Marionette

Here is what you need:

large cereal box and a smaller food box
cardboard egg carton
black paint and a paintbrush
thick string or white shoelaces
regular string
two 12-inch (30-cm) brown pipe cleaners
brown grocery bag
black marker
clear packing tape
scissors
cardboard paper-towel tube
cardboard toilet-tissue tube

The wide hooves of the caribou act like snowshoes, making it easier for them to walk on snow.

Here is what you do:

1. Cut down the seam and around the bottom of the brown grocery bag to get a flat sheet of brown paper.

2. Use packing tape and the brown paper to cover the boxes by wrapping them as you would a present. Leave open the paper at the open end of the two boxes.

3. Cut four separate egg cups from the egg carton. Cut a V-shaped notch in each one to look like the hoof of a caribou. Paint each hoof black.

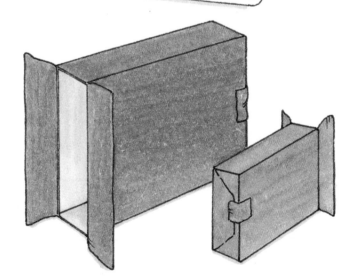

4 You will need two 24-inch (60-cm) shoelaces or pieces of heavy string for the legs. Turn the box on its side for the body of the caribou. Poke a hole on opposite sides of the bottom edge toward the front of the box. Make another set of holes toward the back of the box. Thread one of the strings through each set of holes so that the ends hang down on each side of the body for legs. Poke a hole in the top of each hoof. String one hoof on the end of each leg. Slide them up to the height that you want them, then knot the end of the string to hold the hoof in place. Trim off the excess string from the bottom.

5 Poke two holes in the top of the body. Cut a 6-foot (2-meter) piece of regular string. Thread the string down one hole and up and out the second hole. Thread one end through the paper-towel tube and tie the two ends together. The tube will be one of the holders for the marionette.

6 Close the open end of the box and tape the paper closed over it.

7 Turn the small box on its side for the head of the caribou.

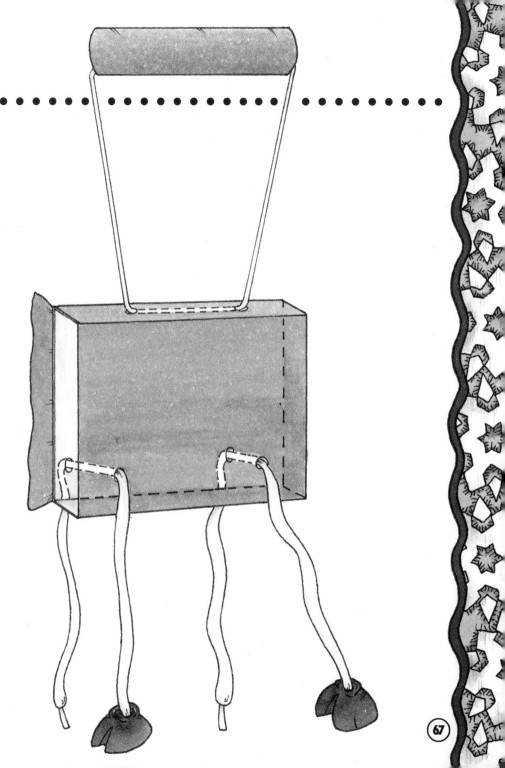

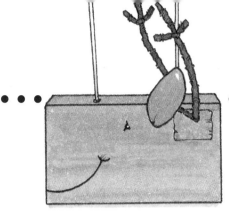

Poke a hole through each side at the top of the open end. Thread a 12-inch (30-cm) pipe cleaner through the hole for the antlers. Cut smaller pieces from the second pipe cleaner to wrap them around the antlers to form the branches. Use packing tape to hold the antlers in an upright position.

Cut two ears from the brown bag scraps. Tape an ear on each side of the head of the caribou.

Use the black marker to draw a face on the front of the head.

Poke two holes in the top of the head. Cut a 5-foot (1.5-meter) piece of string to thread through the two holes. Thread one end of the string through the toilet-tissue tube, then tie the two ends of the string together. The smaller tube will be the holder for the head portion of the marionette.

Close the open end of the smaller box and seal the paper using packing tape.

Cut an 8-inch (20-cm) piece of heavy string or use a shoelace. Tape one end of the string to the head and the other end to the body to join the two pieces together.

Hold one tube of the marionette in each hand and walk the caribou across the floor.

68

Bottled Auroras

Here is what you need:

corn syrup
package of star-shaped sequins
blue or green food coloring
16-ounce (473 ml) plastic soda bottle with a
   twist-on cap

Here is what you do:

1. Wash out the plastic bottle and remove the label.

2. Pour about ½ to one cup of corn syrup into the bottle.

3. Color the corn syrup with about three drops of food coloring.

4. Drop 10 or more stars into the bottle.

5. Put the cap back on the bottle and make sure it is tight.

6. Tip the bottle back and forth to evenly color the corn syrup, then tip the bottle upside-down, then right-side-up to see the colors streak through the sky.

Colorful lights, called auroras, appear in the skies of the polar regions.

If you don't have star-shaped sequins, you can make your own stars by punching them out of aluminum foil using a star-shaped punch.

69

Snowy Owl Chicks Wall Hanging

Here is what you need:

three pinecones of different sizes
fiberfill
white glue
9-inch (23-cm) paper plate
yellow and black paper scraps
blue poster paint and a paintbrush
thin ribbon or yarn
hole punch
scissors
newspaper to work on

The chicks in the nest of a snowy owl will be of different sizes and ages because the owl, unlike most other birds, incubates each egg as it is laid.

Here is what you do:

To make each chick, wrap a pinecone in a thin layer of fiberfill, with the brown petals of the pinecone sticking through.

Cut eyes from yellow paper. Punch pupils from the black paper and glue a pupil in the center of each eye. Glue two eyes on one side of one end of the pinecone.

Cut triangle beaks for the owls from black paper. Glue them in place under the eyes to complete the faces of the owls.

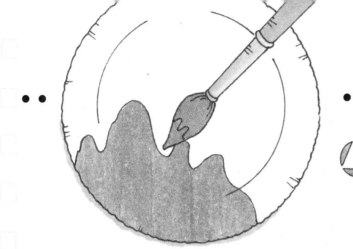

4 Paint the eating side of the paper plate blue. Let the paint dry.

5 Glue the three owl chicks next to each other on the front of the plate. Glue a little bit of fiberfill across the bottom for snow.

6 Punch two holes in the top of the plate. String an 8-inch (20-cm) piece of ribbon through the two holes and tie the ends together to make a hanger for the owls.

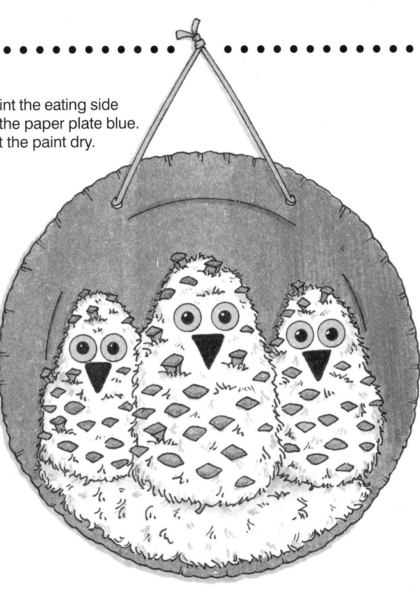

Snowy owls build nests on the ground, but these owls will be very happy on your wall.

Bag Narwhal

Here is what you need:

four large brown grocery bags
long cardboard gift-wrap tube
masking tape
black and white poster paint and a paintbrush
newspaper for stuffing and to work on
white glue
scissors
stapler
paper towels

Male and some female narwhals have a long spiral tusk growing from the upper lip.

Here is what you do:

Stuff the first bag almost to the top with crumpled newspaper. Stuff a second bag about three-quarters full of crumpled newspaper. Slide the bottom of the second bag into the open end of the first bag. Rub glue between the sides of the two bags where they touch to hold them together.

Stuff the bottom quarter of the third bag. Flatten the bag and cut the top three quarters into the shape of a whale tail. Staple the bag shut. Slide the bottom of the bag into the open second bag of the whale so that the tail hangs out at the end. Rub glue between the two bags to hold the tail in place.

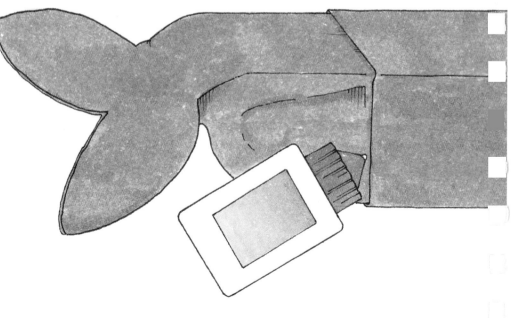

3) Cut two fins for the whale from the last brown bag. Glue a fin on each side of the whale.

4) Paint the entire whale white. While the paint is still wet, use a paper towel to dab black paint all over the white paint to resemble the grayish color of the narwhal.

5) Use the black paint to paint eyes and a mouth at the head of the narwhal.

6) To make the spiral tusk, cut a slit down the cardboard tube almost to the other end. Wrap the cut tube around itself to form the pointed tusk. Use masking tape to hold the wrapped tube in place.

7) Cover the entire tube by wrapping it with masking tape.

8) Cut a hole slightly smaller than the end of the tube just above the mouth. Work the wide end of the tusk into the hole and the stuffing. Take the tusk out, rub the end with glue, then put it back in place in the head of the narwhal.

You will need a large space to display this magnificent creature.

Molting Beluga

Here is what you need:

two white socks
fiberfill
scissors
white glue
black marker
two clamp clothespins

The beluga whale molts, and is thought to rub the old skin off on the ocean floor.

Here is what you do:

Stuff the foot of one white sock with fiberfill. Cut the cuff of the sock into a tail for the whale. Glue the top and bottom side of the tail together. Use clamp clothespins to hold the sock shut until the glue dries.

Cut two fins from the sock cuff scraps. Glue one on each side of the whale.

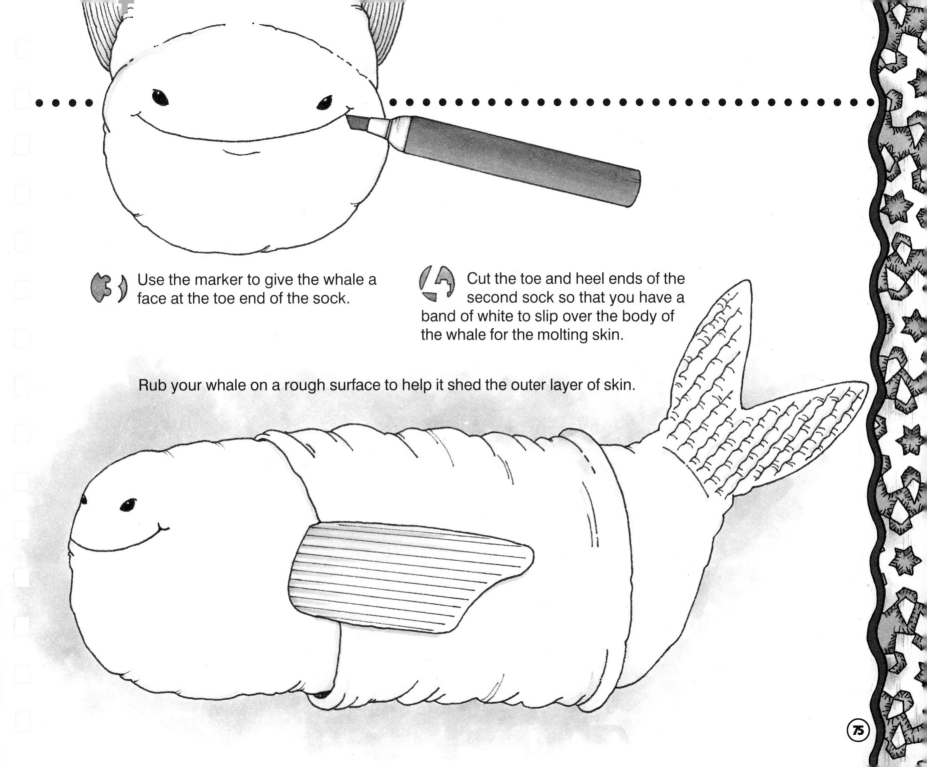

3) Use the marker to give the whale a face at the toe end of the sock.

4) Cut the toe and heel ends of the second sock so that you have a band of white to slip over the body of the whale for the molting skin.

Rub your whale on a rough surface to help it shed the outer layer of skin.

Arctic Fox Cup Puppet

Here is what you need:

two Styrofoam cups
white construction paper scrap
fiberfill
masking tape
white glue
paper fastener
two wiggle eyes
black pom-pom

The arctic fox also has the protective coloration of a changing coat.

Here is what you do:

Cut two triangle-shaped ears in the rim of one cup. Trim away the rest of the rim. Turn the cup on its side for the head of the fox. Bend the ears so that they stick up at the top of the head.

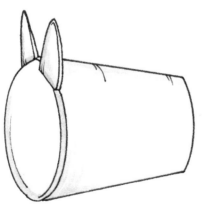

The second cup will be the body cup. Turn the cup upside-down so that the bottom of the cup becomes the neck area of the fox. Attach the head to the body with the paper fastener.

76

3 Cut a tail for the fox from the white paper. Tape the end of the tail inside the bottom, back of the cup body so that it sticks out from the back of the fox.

4 Cover the head and body of the fox with strips of masking tape to create a better gluing surface. Glue fiberfill all over the fox to give it a winter coat.

5 Glue the two wiggle eyes on the head. Glue the black pom-pom on the head for the nose.

You might want to make a second arctic fox wearing a brownish summer coat. Just follow the same instructions and dab the fiberfill coat with brownish paint.

Hands and Foot Arctic Tern

Here is what you need:

white, black, and orange construction paper
pencil
black marker
scissors
white glue

Here is what you do:

The arctic tern travels from the Arctic to the Antarctic and back again each year. This bird holds the record for the longest distance traveled in a year.

1. Trace around your foot on the white paper. Cut out the foot shape to use as the body for your bird.

2. Trace both your hands on the white paper. Cut out four of each hand. Using both of your hands for a pattern instead of just one will give the feathers a more varied look.

3. The heel of the foot shape will be the head of the bird. Cut out a long pointed beak from the orange paper. Glue the end of the beak on the end of the heel of the foot shape.

4 Cut an oval-shaped black cap for the bird. Glue it in the center end of the heel.

5 Use the marker to draw an eye on each edge of the black cap.

6 Glue two hand shapes next to each other and slightly flared out on the back of the bird for a tail.

7 Glue three hand shapes with palms partly overlapping on each side of the bird for wings.

You can mount the arctic tern on blue paper or just tape it to a window or wall as is.

Books About Polar Life

Barrett, Norman S. *Polar Animals.* London: Franklin Watts, 1988.

Bender, Lionel. *Polar Animals.* New York: Gloucester Press, 1989.

Chinery, Michael. *Questions and Answers About Polar Animals.* New York: Kingfisher Books, 1994.

Gilbreath, Alice Thompson. *The Arctic and Antarctica: Roof and Floor of the World.* Minneapolis: Dillon Press, 1988.

Huntington, Lee Pennock. *The Arctic and Antarctic: What Lives There.* New York: Coward, McCann and Geoghegan, 1975.

Johnson, Sylvia A. *Animals of the Polar Regions.* Minneapolis: Lerner Publications Co., 1976.

Khanduri, Kamini. *Polar Wildlife.* London: Usborne Publishing, 1992.

Lambert, David. *Polar Regions.* Morristown, NJ: Silver Burdett Press, 1988.

Pearce, Q.L. *Killer Whales and Other Frozen World Wonders.* Englewood Cliffs, NJ: Messner, 1991.

Pedersen, Alwin. *Polar Animals.* New York: Taplinger Pub. Co., 1966.

Sandak, Cass R. *The Arctic and Antarctic.* New York: Franklin Watts, 1987.

Taylor, Barbara. *Arctic and Antarctic.* New York: Knopf, Distributed by Random House, 1995.

Rainforests

Rainforests are the thick tangle of trees and plants that grow in the warm, wet lands near the equator. These forests make up less than one twentieth of the earth's land, but scientists believe that the plants and animals found in the rainforests account for more than half the species found on this planet.

It is estimated that about one thousand different groups of people live in tropical forests. Many medicines come from the trees and plants found only in the rainforests. The rainforests are also an important source of oxygen for our planet, and they affect weather and earth's atmosphere, too. Yet people's destruction of the rainforests continues—and we lose 50 million acres (20 million hectares) of this valuable land each year.

This section contains models of just a few of the amazing number of plants and animals that are part of the rainforests. The Rainforest Layers model would make an impressive introduction to any science presentation having to do with the rainforests. Some of the more interesting creatures are the Tree Frog Beanbag, Common Iguana, and the Fruit Bat.

Add more details to your projects or give them more accurate coloring by looking for pictures and more information on the plants and animals you make. Learning more about rainforests is an essential step in understanding the importance of saving them. There's a listing of some of the many books available on the rainforests on page 104.

Rainforest Layers

Here is what you need:

large jar with lid
modeling clay
brown tissue paper
two or more shades of green tissue paper
sticks and twigs
Easter grass
white glue
masking tape
marker

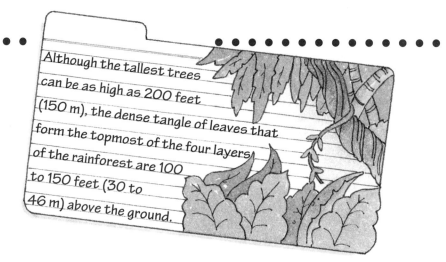

Although the tallest trees can be as high as 200 feet (150 m), the dense tangle of leaves that form the topmost of the four layers of the rainforest are 100 to 150 feet (30 to 46 m) above the ground.

Here is what you do:

Press a ball of clay onto the inside surface of the jar lid. Do not press it onto the sides of the lid, because you will not be able to put the lid back on the jar.

Break two sticks so that they are as long as the jar. Press them into the clay to make trees. Crumple some green or brown tissue paper and glue it around the top of the sticks to make the leaves. These tall trees are found in the emergent layer of the rainforest.

Break two or three more sticks so that they are about three-quarters the size of the first trees. Press these shorter trees, which form the rainforest's canopy layer, into the clay around the tall trees. Crumple tissue to glue around the top of the short sticks to make the leaves.

4 Break two or three thin twigs so that they are about half the size of the second trees. These twigs form the young trees and shrubs found in the understory of the rainforest. Cut some long, narrow leaves from green tissue paper and glue them to the tops of the twigs.

5 Crumple a piece of brown tissue paper and glue it over the clay around the base of the trees. This forms the carpet of moss and dead leaves that make up the forest floor.

6 Wrap strands of Easter grass around the tree to make vines.

7 When the glue has dried, carefully slip the jar over the trees and screw the lid on.

8 With the marker, write the name of each of the four layers of the rainforest on a strip of masking tape. Stick the labels on the jar to mark each layer.

Many animals spend their entire lives in just one layer of the rainforest.

83

Necktie Bromeliad

Here is what you need:

4 old neckties
plastic cap from fabric-softener bottle
3 rubber bands
white glue
scissors
green poster paint and paintbrush
blue tissue paper or plastic wrap
colorful construction paper scraps
markers
Styrofoam tray to work on

There are about 1,500 types of bromeliads, including Spanish moss and the pineapple plant. The leaf clusters of many bromeliads form a cup that catches rainwater.

Here is what you do:

Cut a piece off the thin end of each necktie about 3 inches (8 cm) long. These pieces will be the inner leaves of the plant. Turn the cap upside down so that it forms a cup. Arrange the four tie pieces around the cap, with the points up. Wrap a rubber band around the ties to hold them in place.

Cut seven or more pieces from the ties. Each should be about 4 inches (10 cm) long. Cut one end of each piece into a point.

3 Rub glue around the inner leaves along the sides of the cup. Stick a layer of longer tie pieces to the shorter ones, points facing outward, using a rubber band to hold them in place.

4 Cut nine or ten more pieces from the ties. Each should be about 5 inches (13 cm) long. Cut one end of each piece into a point.

5 Rub glue around the outer leaves along the sides of the cup. Stick a layer of long tie pieces to them, using another rubber band to hold them all in place.

6 Paint all of the necktie leaves green and let the plant dry on the Styrofoam tray.

7 Crumple some blue plastic wrap or tissue paper and put it inside the cup. Now you have water in the little pond.

8 Cut some insects out of colorful paper and draw details with the markers. Glue the insects to the leaves of the bromeliad plant.

You can also cut out some pollywogs to live in the water.

"Hand"Some Orchids

Here is what you need for each flower:

green pipe cleaner, 12 inches (30 cm) long
orange pipe cleaner, 4 inches (10 cm) long
construction paper in green and a
    bright color of your choice
pencil
scissors
cellophane tape

Here is what you do:

Trace both of your hands on the bright-colored paper. Trace one hand on the green paper. Cut out the three tracings.

Bend the orange pipe cleaner in half. Wrap one end of the green pipe cleaner around the bend, to make a stem for the flower. Bend each end of the orange pipe cleaner outward to make the stamen of the flower.

Wrap the two bright-colored hands around the stamen. Tape them in place to form the petals of the flower.

Wrap the green hand around the stamen, just below the other petals. Tape it in place to form the leaves.

There are more than 20,000 species of orchids in the world. They come in every color except black.

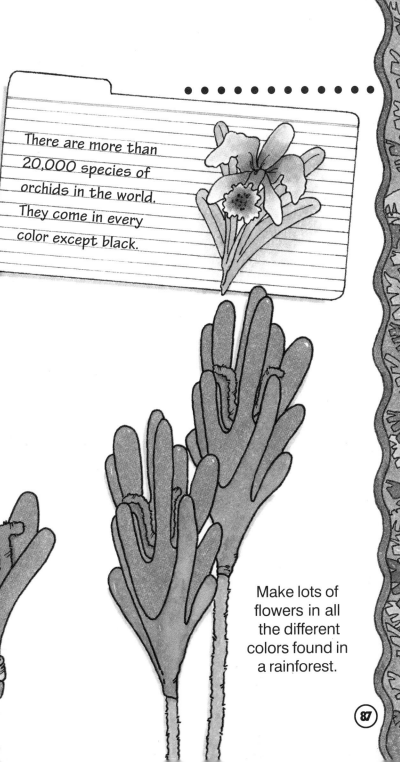

Make lots of flowers in all the different colors found in a rainforest.

87

Common Iguana

Here is what you need:

two cardboard toilet-tissue tubes
one cardboard paper-towel tube
cereal-box cardboard
green tissue paper
orange construction paper
black marker
masking tape
green and orange poster paint and paintbrush
scissors
newspaper to work on

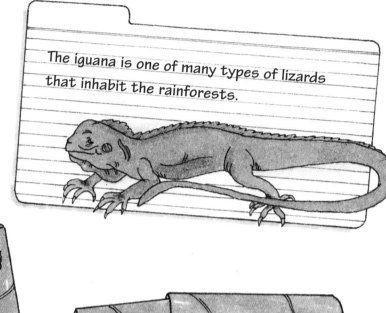

The iguana is one of many types of lizards that inhabit the rainforests.

Here is what you do:

Cut a slit 3 inches (8 cm) long in the toilet-tissue tubes. Overlap the cut edges to form a cone shape. Use masking tape to hold the edges in place. This will be the head of the iguana.

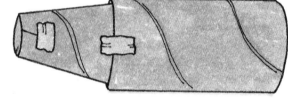

Cut a slit in the other side of the head. Overlap the cut edges just enough so that the end of the cone fits inside one end of the other toilet-tissue tube. Tape the two tubes together. They form the head and body of the iguana.

Cut a slit in the paper-towel tube, leaving 1 inch (2.5 cm) uncut at one end. Overlap the edges of the tube to form a long cone shape. This is the iguana's tail. Tape the cone shape to hold it in place.

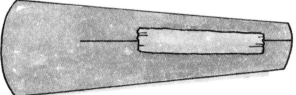

88

4 Cut a small slit in the other end of the tail tube. Overlap the edges just enough so that the end of the cone fits inside the open end of the body. Tape the tail to the body.

5 Cut four legs for the iguana from the cardboard. Glue the legs on each side of the iguana's body. Let the glue dry.

6 Paint the iguana green. Dab a little orange paint over the green paint on each foot.

7 Cut tiny eyes from the orange paper. With the marker, draw a pupil in each eye. Glue the eyes on the iguana's head.

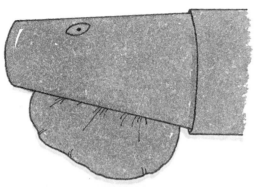

Cut a piece of green tissue paper, 2 inches (5 cm) by 3 inches (8 cm). Round off the edges of the paper. An iguana has skin that hangs down under its chin. Gather one side of the paper slightly. Glue the gathered side under the iguana's chin.

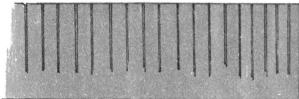

Cut a strip of paper 2 inches (5 cm) wide and as long as the iguana, from its head to its tail. Cut fringe along the length of one edge of the paper. Glue the other edge of the paper to the iguana, so that the fringe sticks up. Trim the fringe so that it is longest at the head and shortest at the tail.

Make some rainforest insects for your iguana to eat.

Spotted Cats

Here is what you need:

orange, white, and light-green construction paper
black and orange paint and paintbrush
markers
white glue
scissors

Here is what you do:

For each cat you wish to make, paint your hand orange and make a handprint on the white construction paper. Cut out all the handprints.

For each hand body, cut out a cat's head from the orange paper. With markers, draw a face on each head. Turn your handprints upside down and glue a head to the palm, opposite the thumb. The thumb forms the tail of the cat, and the fingers form the legs.

Dip your finger in black paint and give each cat lots of spots.

With the markers, draw a rainforest environment for the cats on the light-green construction paper. Glue the cats on the rainforest picture.

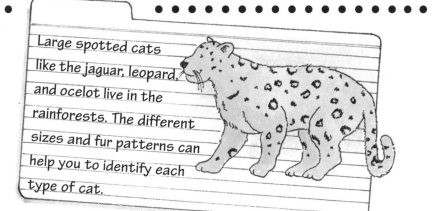

Large spotted cats like the jaguar, leopard, and ocelot live in the rainforests. The different sizes and fur patterns can help you to identify each type of cat.

Find pictures of different species of big cats and fill your rainforest with them.

91

Tree Frog Beanbag

Here is what you need:

old red adult-size sock
dark-blue felt
two white 1-inch (2.5-cm) pom-poms
dried beans
plastic sandwich bag
hole punch
scissors
white glue
clamp clothespin

Many kinds of brightly colored frogs live in the rainforest. You might want to use a different color for each frog you make.

Here is what you do:

Cut a piece off the foot of the sock, about 5 inches (13 cm) from the toe. The cut piece will be the body of the frog.

Pour enough dried beans into the sock to fill it about three-quarters full. Dump the beans into the plastic bag. Fold over the open end of the bag and put the bag in the sock.

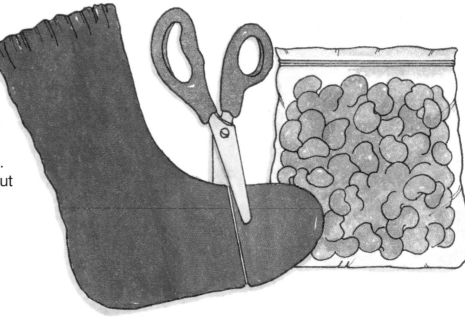

3. Cut front and back legs for the frog from the blue felt.

4. Fold in the edge of the open end of the sock. Rub glue along the folded edges. Put the two back legs of the frog between the top and bottom of the opening. Attach clothespins to hold the opening together until the glue dries.

5. Glue the front legs underneath the other end of the frog's body.

6. Glue the two white pom-poms on the top front of the body to make the eyes. Punch two holes out of the blue felt. Glue one dot on the center of each pom-pom.

When the glue has dried, your frog beanbag is ready to play with.

Hummingbird and Flower Puppets

Here is what you need:

old knit adult-size glove
flexi-straw
craft feathers
two tiny wiggle eyes
pink felt
yellow, blue, and green poster paint and paintbrush
white glue
scissors

Here is what you do:

Cut off two fingers of the knit glove to use for the puppets.

Paint the tip of one glove finger yellow to make the center of the flower finger puppet. Cut a flower shape about 5 inches (13 cm) wide from the pink felt. Cut a slit 1 inch (2.5 cm) wide in the center of the flower and slip the flower over the painted tip of the finger. Cut a second flower shape about 4 inches (10 cm) wide. Cut a slit 1 inch (2.5 cm) wide in the center of that flower. Slip the second flower on top of the first one to complete your flower finger puppet.

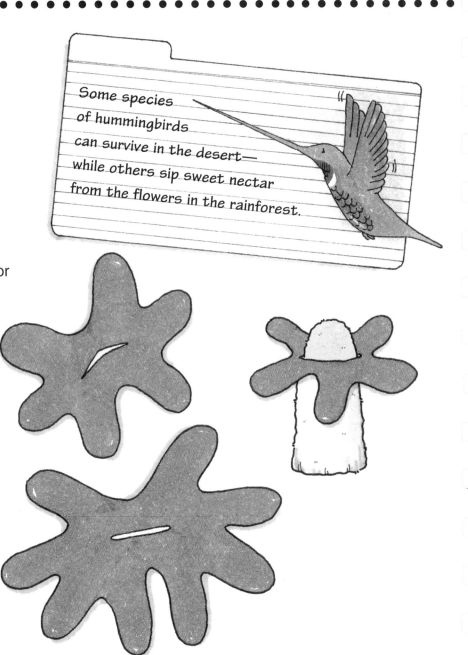

Some species of hummingbirds can survive in the desert—while others sip sweet nectar from the flowers in the rainforest.

To make the hummingbird puppet, paint the other glove finger with blue and green paint.

Cut a tiny slit in the tip of the glove finger. Slide the top end of the flexi-straw into the bottom of the glove finger and out the tiny slit. Bend the straw to form the long beak of the hummingbird. The other end of the straw is a holder for the puppet.

Glue two tiny wiggle eyes to the head of the bird. Glue on colorful craft feathers to make the outspread wings and the tail of the bird.

Put the flower puppet on the finger of one of your hands. With the other hand, fly the hummingbird over for a sip of nectar.

Window Toucan

Here is what you need:

small sheet of light-green construction paper
black and light-blue construction paper
yellow, green, orange, and red tissue paper
red yarn
hole punch
scissors
white glue
pencil

Although the toucan has become a symbol of the rainforest, there are 131 species, many of which live in other habitats.

Here is what you do:

Turn the light-green paper so that its longest edges are at the top and bottom. With the pencil, sketch a large toucan beak on the paper. Cut out the beak shape, without cutting through any of the sides of the paper.

Cut a half circle out of the black paper to make the head of the toucan. Glue the straight edge of the half circle to the edge of the green paper. The curved side of the half circle should slightly overlap the widest part of the beak.

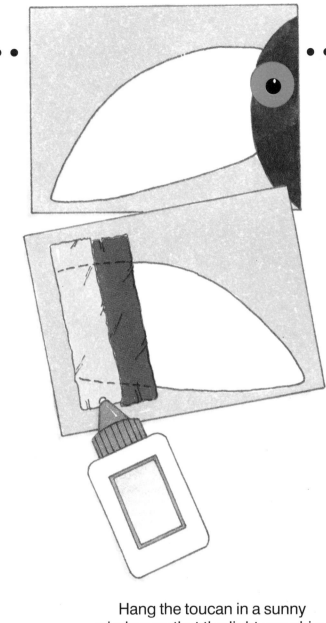

3 Cut an eye from the blue paper and a pupil from the black paper. Glue the pupil in the center of the eye. Glue the eye on the head of the toucan.

4 Cut strips of colorful tissue. Glue the strips across the back of the paper to fill in the opening you made when you cut out the toucan's beak. Cut as many tissue-paper strips as you need to fill the entire opening.

5 Punch a hole close to each side of the top of the paper. Cut a long piece of yarn. Thread the yarn through the two holes and tie the ends together to make a hanger for the toucan.

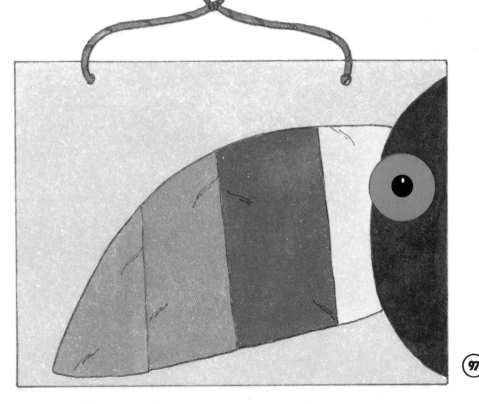

Hang the toucan in a sunny window so that the light can shine through the colorful beak.

Foot and Hands Macaw

Here is what you need:

construction paper in several bright colors
black construction paper scrap
pencil
scissors

Here is what you do:

1. Trace around your shoe on a piece of brightly colored paper. Cut the shoe shape out to use for the body of the bird, with the heel end forming the head.

2. Cut two black eyes and glue them to the head. Cut a curved beak from yellow paper and glue it below the bird's eyes. Cut out two claw feet from the black paper. Glue the feet to the bottom of the bird.

Macaws are very beautiful parrots, but they are not often kept as pets as they tend to scream rather than talk—and they may bite!

3 Trace around your hand on a different color of paper than you used for the body of the bird. Stack the paper on three other colors of paper and cut the hand shape out. Glue the four hand shapes together in a row with the fingers of each hand hanging down below the fingers of the hand above it to form a tail. Glue the tail to the back bottom of the bird so that the fingers hang down to look like tail feathers.

4 Stack two pieces of each of three different colors of paper. Trace your hand on the top piece of paper. Cut the hand shape out. Glue three different color hand shapes together in the same way you glued the tail, to make each of the bird's wings. Glue one wing on the bird sticking out from behind the left side. Glue the other wing to the front of the bird and sticking out from the right side.

You can be creative with the colors you use for your bird or you can copy one of the color combinations of a real macaw. You can find pictures of different macaws at the library.

Fruit Bat

Here is what you need:

old adult-size brown sock
brown construction paper
black marker
scissors
white glue
wire hanger
5 black pipe cleaners, each 12 inches (30 cm) long
fiberfill
old pantyhose
three large safety pins
masking tape

Fruit-eating bats spread seeds throughout rainforests, thus helping the plants to regenerate.

Here is what you do:

Cut off the cuff of the sock. To make the bat's body, stuff the foot of the sock with fiberfill. Close the sock by wrapping half a pipe cleaner tightly around the opening. Bend the two ends of the pipe cleaner to make the bat's legs. Cut two pieces of pipe cleaner 1 inch (2.5 cm) long. Wrap one short piece of pipe cleaner around each leg, about 3/4 inch (2 cm) from the end. Bend all the pipe-cleaner ends to make toes for the bat.

Cut ears, eyes, and nose holes from the brown paper. With the marker, add pupils to the eyes. Glue the features to the front of the bat to make its face.

3) To make wings for the bat, wrap pipe cleaners back and forth across the inside of the wire hanger to make a network of bones.

4) Cut off one leg of the pantyhose. Slip the cutoff leg over the hanger. Poke the hook of the hanger through the middle of the stocking. Make a knot in each end of the stocking, making sure it is pulled tightly across the hanger. Trim off any extra stocking around the knots.

5) Pin the wings to the back of the bat with safety pins. Make sure the hook end of the hanger is behind the bat's feet. Squeeze the hook of the hanger closer together and tape the end with masking tape so that it is not sharp.

Find a good place for your fruit bat to hang around.

Howling Howler Monkey Mask

Here is what you need:

cardboard paper-towel tube
paper plate, 9 inches (23 cm) in diameter
two paper plates, 7 inches (18 cm) in diameter
black, brown, and white construction-paper scraps
reddish brown yarn
black poster paint and paintbrush
white glue
scissors
newspaper to work on

The call of the howler monkey can be heard up to a mile and a half (2.5 km) away.

Here is what you do:

1 Cut six slits 1 1/2 inches (4 cm) long around one end of the cardboard tube. Bend all the cut pieces away from the tube.

2 Near the edge of the large plate, trace around the uncut end of the tube. Cut out the traced circle.

3 Trace another circle in the middle of the bottom half of one of the small plates. Cut out the circle. Stack the two small plates together and use the hole in the first plate to trace a circle on the second small plate. Cut that circle out, too.

4 Push the uncut end of the tube through the hole in one of the small plates, from the underside of the plate to the top. Push the tube through until the cut pieces rest on the bottom of the plate. Rub glue all over the bottom of the plate and the cut ends of the tube. Press the other small plate on top of the glue. Be sure to match the holes in both of the plates.

102

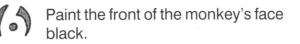

5 Slide the large plate over the tube, so that the bottom of the large plate rests on the two small plates. The large plate forms the monkey's head, and the smaller plates form the monkey's muzzle. Glue the larger plate to the smaller plates.

6 Paint the front of the monkey's face black.

7 Cut eyes, ears, and a nose from the construction-paper scraps and glue them in place.

8 To make fur, cut lots of snips of yarn, about 1 inch (2.5 cm) long. Glue them all over the head of the monkey and around the muzzle.

Howl and bark through the tube, just like a noisy howler monkey.

Books About Rainforests

Cherry, Lynne. *The Great Kapok Tree.* Orlando, FL: Harcourt Brace & Co., 1990.

Cowcher, Helen. *Rain Forest.* New York: Farrar, Straus, & Giroux, Inc., 1988.

Darling, Kathy. *Rain Forest Babies.* New York: Walker Publishing, 1996.

Dunphy, Madeline. *Here Is the Tropical Rainforest.* New York: Hyperion Books for Children, 1994.

Gibbons, Gail. *Nature's Green Umbrella: Tropical Rain Forests.* New York: Morrow Junior Books, 1994.

Jeunese, Gillimand and Mettler, Rene. *The Rain Forest.* New York: Scholastic, Inc., 1994.

Jordan, Martin and Tanis. *Journey of the Red-Eyed Tree Frog.* New York: Green Tiger Press, 1992.

Lepthien, Emilie. *Tropical Rainforests.* Danbury, CT: Childrens Press, 1993.

Lessen, Don. *Inside the Amazing Amazon.* New York: Crown Publishing Group, 1995.

Patent, Dorothy Hinshaw. *Children Save the Rainforest.* New York: Cobble Hill Books, 1996.

Ricciuti, Edward. *Rainforest.* Tarrytown, NY: Marshall Cavendish, 1994.

Ryder, Joanne and Rothman, Michael. *Jaguar in the Rain Forest.* New York: Morrow Junior Books, 1996.

Sayre, April. *Tropical Rainforest.* New York: Twenty-First Century Books, 1994.

Sirace, Carolyn. *Rainforest.* Austin, TX: Steck-Vaughn, 1994.

Warburton, Lois. *Rain Forest.* San Diego, CA: Lucent Books, Inc., 1991.

Willow, Diane. *At Home in the Rainforest.* Watertown, MA: Charlesbridge Publishing, 1991.

Yolen, Jane. *Welcome to the Greenhouse.* New York: Scholastic, Inc., 1994.

Insects

All the creatures that I have included in this section are true insects. They meet the definition of an insect: three main body parts—a head, a thorax, and an abdomen; antennae on top of the head, six legs, and an outer shell that protects the soft insides. Many insects have compound eyes, meaning they have many lenses in each eye instead of just one. I have not added compound eyes on all the models, but you may want to for the sake of accuracy.

Insects are fascinating creatures. What I have tried to do in this section is to feature one interesting trait for each insect I made. Some impressive models include the Hungry Mosquito (you can actually see it draw blood from a sponge hand!), the Jumping Grasshopper, and the Worker Ant. Teachers will love the Butterfly Metamorphosis demonstration.

If you want to learn more about insects, I've suggested some interesting books on page 128.

Lucky Ladybug Necklace

Here is what you need:

two pry-off bottle caps
red nail polish
sharp black permanent marker
black felt scrap
black yarn
scissors
white glue
a lucky penny

Some people say that ladybugs bring good luck. Maybe it is because they eat insects that are harmful to crops and gardens.

Here is what you do:

Paint the outside of both bottle caps with red nail polish and let the polish dry.

 Cut a small strip of black felt. Glue one end inside each cap to form a hinge that will allow the caps to open and close, forming a locket.

Cut a circle of black felt to fit inside one of the caps and glue it in place.

106

4 Use lots of glue to glue your lucky penny inside the other cap. Let the glue dry overnight.

5 Use the black marker to draw the head and spots of the ladybug on the cap with the felt inside it.

6 Cut a piece of black yarn, about 2 feet (60 cm) long, on which to hang your ladybug. Thread the yarn around the hinge and tie the two ends together.

Perhaps the hidden penny will make your ladybug extra lucky!

Butterfly Lapel Pin

Here is what you need:

two colorful old neckties
orange or yellow pipe cleaner
two tiny wiggle eyes
white glue
scissors
safety pin

When a butterfly hatches, it must pump liquid into its wings to make them expand.

Here is what you do:

Cut a 4-inch (10-cm) piece from the narrow end of each necktie, measuring from the tip of the point. Cut the flat end of each piece into a point to match the sewn point of the tie.

Set one piece over the other piece to form an X-shape with both cut points at the bottom.

Cut a 6-inch (15-cm) piece of pipe cleaner. Fold the pipe cleaner in half over the center of the X so that the pipe cleaner forms the body of the butterfly and the tie pieces form the wings. Pinch the center of the wings together slightly, then wrap the two ends of the pipe cleaner around each other to form the antennae of the butterfly.

Glue two tiny wiggle eyes below the antennae.

Slide the safety pin through the back of the pipe cleaner body and the butterfly is ready to wear.

Caterpillar-to-Butterfly Puppet

Here is what you need:

two pairs of colored or patterned shoulder pads
two old adult sport socks with colored stripes
adult-size brown sock
1-inch (2.5-cm) safety pin
yellow paper scrap
black marker
scissors
white glue

A caterpillar's first meal is the shell of the egg it hatches from. In one day, a caterpillar can eat several times its weight in leaves.

cross-section of a cocoon

Here is what you do:

Arrange the four shoulder pads into two separate sets of butterfly wings. Pin one set just behind the other on the bottom of the foot of the brown sock, about halfway between the heel and the toe. (If the shoulder pads have Velcro on them, it would be good to remove it, so it won't stick to the sock when you turn it inside out.)

Cut two eyes from the yellow paper. Draw a black dot in the center of each eye. Glue the two eyes to the top of the butterfly. Let the glue dry before continuing.

To make the caterpillar, turn the sock inside out so that the butterfly wings are inside.

Cut three or more striped bands from the sport socks to slip over the brown sock for caterpillar stripes. Glue the stripes in place.

Cut two eyes from the yellow paper. Draw a black dot in the center of each eye. Glue the eyes on the bottom of the toe end of the sock. Let the glue dry completely before you use the puppet.

You can change your caterpillar to a butterfly by turning the sock puppet inside out.

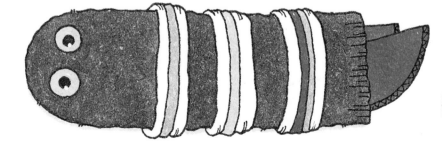

Flashing Firefly Puppet

Here is what you need:

adult-size brown sock with 8 to 9 inches (20 to 23 cm) of ribbing
two brown buttons
four 12-inch (30-cm) orange pipe cleaners
white tissue paper
white glue
scissors
green see-through disposable plastic cup
flashlight
rubber band

Fireflies flash to each other with their lights.

Here is what you do:

Cut the foot off the sock. The ribbed part will be the body of the firefly.

Put the top of the sock over the rim of the cup. Hold the cup in place with a rubber band. Fold about 1 inch (2.5 cm) of the top of the sock over the rubber band to conceal it.

Glue two brown buttons on one side of the other end of the sock for the eyes.

4. Turn the sock over to the other side. Thread three of the pipe cleaners through the side of the sock about halfway down. Bend the pipe cleaners to form the six legs of the firefly.

5. Cut a 6-inch (15-cm) piece of pipe cleaner. Thread it through the sock above the eyes to make antennae. Bend the two antennae into a curved shape.

6. Cut four wings from white tissue paper. Glue the wings to the firefly. Let the glue dry completely.

To use your firefly puppet, slip your hand and a flashlight into the sock body. Flash the light on and off to call other fireflies. The green cup will give your puppet a green glow in the dark.

Hungry Mosquito

Here is what you need:

eyedropper
brown pipe cleaner
three hairpins
used white dryer sheet
two tiny wiggle eyes
white glue
scissors
pink sponge
black permanent marker
red food coloring
1/2 cup (125 ml) water
small shallow dish

Male mosquitoes feed on plant nectar, but females prefer to bite you for a meal of blood. Yuck!

Here is what you do:

To make the mosquito, wrap the brown pipe cleaner around the tube of the eyedropper, leaving the tip exposed.

Wrap the three hairpins around the body between the pipe cleaners to form the legs. Bend the legs out, then downward, about halfway down each leg. Rub glue over the place where the legs and pipe cleaner touch.

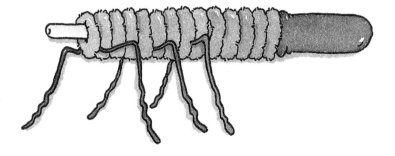

3 Cut two wings from the dryer sheet. Glue the wings on the back of the mosquito. Glue the two wiggle eyes at the dropper tip end of the mosquito.

4 With the permanent marker, draw a hand shape on the sponge. Cut the hand out and place it in the shallow dish.

Mix some "blood" for the mosquito by adding a few drops of red food coloring to the 1/2 cup of water. Pour the "blood" on the sponge hand and let it absorb the liquid. Bring the mosquito in for a landing on the hand, bury the dropper nose in the sponge, squeeze the bulb of the eyedropper, and watch the mosquito get a meal.

Jumping Grasshopper

Here is what you need:

cardboard egg carton
yellow and green construction paper
black marker
green paint and a paintbrush
1 1/2-inch (3 3/4-cm) rubber ball
two straight pins
scissors
white glue
newspaper to work on

A grasshopper is able to jump about twenty times its own body length. Wow! What if you could do that?

Here is what you do:

Cut a row of three attached cups from the egg carton.

Paint the outside of the cups green and let the paint dry.

Place the ball inside the middle cup. Push a straight pin into the ball through each side of the cup to hold the ball in place.

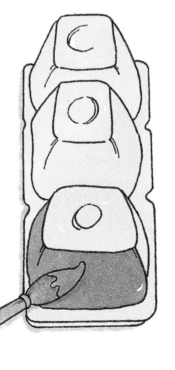

4 Cut three pairs of legs for the grasshopper from the green paper. Glue the legs to the middle segment of the insect, with the front legs going forward and the other four legs going backward. Cut wings from the green paper and glue them to the back of the grasshopper.

5 Cut two eyes from the yellow paper. If you wish, draw a dot in the center of each eye. (A grasshopper's eye does not really have a single pupil.)

To make the grasshopper hop, hold it a few inches above a hard surface and drop it. Don't let it get away!

Flea Game

Here is what you need:

large-size oatmeal box
large brown or black ribbed sock
white, red, and black construction paper scraps
two 1 1/2-inch (3 3/4-cm) black or brown pom-poms
scissors
white glue
brown tissue paper
black marker
one or more 1 1/2-inch (3 3/4-cm) rubber balls

Forty million years ago when a giant woolly mammoth lumbered by, there were fleas waiting to hop on board!

Here is what you do:

Pull the cuff of the brown sock up over the oatmeal box to cover it. Cut the excess sock off at the foot end.

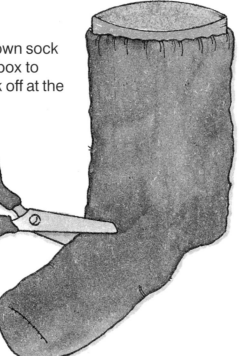

Cut two long, floppy dog ears from the foot of the sock. Glue them on each side of the top of the oatmeal box.

Cut eyes for the dog from the white paper. Add some black pupils, and then glue the eyes near the top front of the box between the ears.

Cut a tongue for the dog from the red paper. Glue it on below the eyes. Glue the two pom-poms above the tongue to shape the dog's muzzle.

To make each flea, cut a piece of brown tissue large enough to cover the ball. Wrap it around the ball and glue the ends together on one side. Trim off the excess tissue. Use the black marker to give the flea a face and legs. Let the glue dry.

Fleas just love to hop onto dogs. Can you hop a flea into the top of the dog you made? Or, try hopping the flea and use the dog container to try to catch it.

Hunting Dragonfly

Here is what you need:

thick green pipe cleaner, 12 inches (30 cm) long
brown pipe cleaner
clear Con-Tact paper
ten tiny wiggle eyes
white thread
green yarn
scissors
pencil
white glue

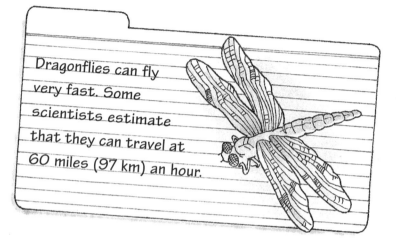

Dragonflies can fly very fast. Some scientists estimate that they can travel at 60 miles (97 km) an hour.

Here is what you do:

1. On the paper side of the Con-Tact paper, use the pencil to sketch two wings attached at the center and about 7 inches (18 cm) long. Stack up four pieces of Con-Tact paper and cut out four double wings.

2. Cut about twenty 6- to 8-inch (15- to 20-cm) pieces of thread. Peel the paper off one of the wings and cover the sticky side with a web of crisscrossed threads. Peel the paper off a second wing piece and stick it directly over the thread-covered wing. Trim the excess threads and Con-Tact paper from around the wings so that the top and bottom pieces match exactly. Then make another set of wings.

3 Bend the green pipe cleaner in half. Twist the folded end to form a head.

4 Cut three 2 1/2-inch (6-cm) pieces of brown pipe cleaner for the legs. Slip them between the folded green pipe cleaner just below the head. Slip the two wings in behind the legs. Twist the remainder of the green pipe cleaner to form the long body of the dragonfly and to hold the wings and legs in place. Bend the legs down and forward to form the leg "basket" a dragonfly uses to catch other insects for dinner.

5 Glue five tiny eyes on each side of the head to represent the compound eyes. A dragonfly actually has 28,000 lenses!

6 Thread a long piece of green yarn through the pipe cleaner body above the wings of the dragonfly. You can hang the insect from the ceiling or fly it around.

You might want to slip a small plastic bug in the leg basket of your dragonfly.

Worker Ant

Here is what you need:

three 2 1/2-inch (6-cm) Styrofoam balls
adult-size black sock
black yarn
four 12-inch (30-cm) black pipe cleaners
two yellow thumbtacks
black permanent marker
piece of white packing Styrofoam
scissors

An ant can lift a weight 50 times as heavy as its own body.

Here is what you do:

Push the three Styrofoam balls into the foot of the black sock so that they are in a row. Push them all the way to the toe of the sock. Tie the opening of the sock shut with a piece of black yarn, as close to the last Styrofoam ball as you can. Trim off the excess sock and the ends of the black yarn.

Tie a piece of black yarn between each Styrofoam ball to define the segments of the body. Trim off the ends of the tied pieces of yarn.

Cut three of the 12-inch-long black pipe cleaners in half so that you have six 6-inch (15-cm) pieces. Push three pieces into each side of the middle segment of the ant to make the legs. Bend each leg down in the middle.

Break off a 1-inch (2 1/2-cm) piece of packing Styrofoam to make a sugar grain for the ant to carry. Push the end of each front leg into each side of the Styrofoam so that the ant is holding the grain.

Cut two 3-inch (7 1/2-cm) pieces of black pipe cleaner. Push each piece into the top of the head to make the antennae.

Push the two yellow thumbtacks into the front of the head to make the eyes. Use the black marker to draw a dot in the center of each tack.

Ants live together in big colonies. Maybe you should make lots of ants!

123

Venus's Flytrap and Fly Puppets

Here is what you need:

two white cotton work gloves
orange felt
adult-size brown sock
green poster paint
paintbrush
scissors
white glue
black glove
white dryer sheet
two tiny wiggle eyes
Styrofoam tray for drying

Some plants eat insects!

Here is what you do:

Paint both work gloves green. Let them dry on the Styrofoam tray.

Cut the toe off the brown sock.

Glue the two work gloves together at the bottom cuff only, with the palms facing in.

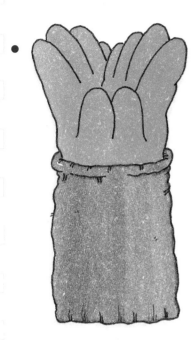

Rub glue around the outside of the two gloves up to the fingers, then pull the cut end of the sock up around the two gloves to form the stem of the plant.

Cut two 3-inch (7 1/2-cm) square pieces of felt. Glue them down in between the two gloves to form the inner lining of the plant.

To make the fly, cut a finger off the black glove. Glue two wiggle eyes at the tip of the finger. Cut wings from the dryer sheet and glue them on the finger behind the eyes.

To use your Venus's-flytrap puppet, slip your hand into one glove of the plant. Put the fly on a finger of your other hand. When the fly touches the sensitive plant, snap your hand shut and your plant will have its dinner.

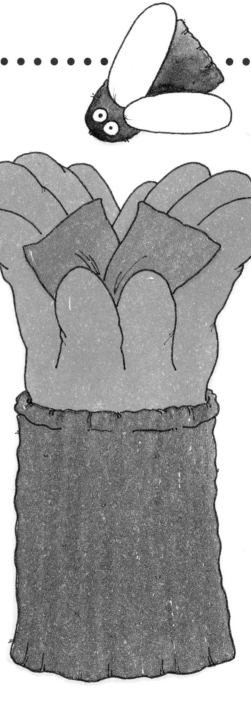

Scurrying Cockroach

Here is what you need:

tiny toy car about 1 1/2 to 2 inches
(3 3/4 to 5 cm) long
black and brown felt
white glue
plastic cup
craft stick
rubber band
scissors
water
two tiny wiggle eyes
thin wire
masking tape
Styrofoam tray for drying

Roaches have been around since before the dinosaurs.

Here is what you do:

Cover the top and sides of the car with masking tape to create a better gluing surface.

Cut a piece of black felt large enough to cover the top and sides of the car.

Mix about 1/2 cup (125 ml) of glue with a few drops of water in the cup. Use the craft stick to stir the mixture well.

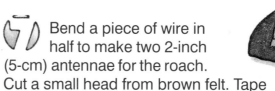

4 Working on the Styrofoam tray, put the felt in the watery glue and mix it around until it is totally covered with glue on both sides. Squeeze the excess glue out of the felt and shape it over the top and sides of the car. Hold the felt in place over the car with the rubber band.

5 Trim off the extra felt around the bottom of the car.

6 Let the car dry completely on a Styrofoam tray. When it is dry, remove the rubber band.

7 Bend a piece of wire in half to make two 2-inch (5-cm) antennae for the roach. Cut a small head from brown felt. Tape the antennae to the underside of the head, then glue the head to one end of the roach body. Curve the two wire antennae out and slightly around.

8 Glue two tiny wiggle eyes to the front of the insect.

When the glue has dried, the roach will be ready to scurry across your kitchen floor.

Books About Insects

Bourgoing, Pascale de. *The Ladybug and Other Insects.* New York: Scholastic, 1991.

Facklam, Margery. *The Big Bug Book.* Boston: Little, Brown, 1993.

Gaffney, Michael. *Secret Forests.* Racine, WI: Golden Books, 1994.

Insects. New York: Dorling Kindersley, 1992.

Kalman, Bobbie. *Bugs and Other Insects.* New York: Crabtree, 1994.

Macquitty, Miranda. *Amazing Bugs.* New York: Dorling Kindersley, 1996.

McGavin, George. *Insects of North America.* San Diego: Thunder Bay Press, 1995.

Mound, L.A. *Insects.* New York: Dorling Kindersley, 1995.

Parker, Jane. *Focus on Insects.* London: Gloucester Press, 1993.

Parker, Nancy Winslow. *Bugs.* New York: Greenwillow Books, 1987.

Parker, Steve. *Beastly Bugs.* Austin, TX: Raintree Steck-Vaughn, 1994.

Richardson, Joy. *Insects.* New York: Franklin Watts, 1993.

Russo, Monica. *The Insect Almanac.* New York: Sterling, 1991.

Wechsler, Doug. *Bizarre Bugs.* New York: Cobblehill Books, 1995.

Woelflein, Luise. *The Ultimate Bug Book.* New York: Western, 1993.

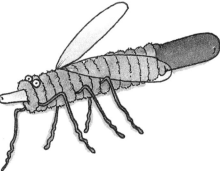

Deserts

When you hear the word desert, you are apt to think of a very hot, sandy, and lifeless place, but this is not always so. Deserts can also be rocky or have a surface of dried mud and salt, called a "pan." There are very cold deserts as well as hot ones. The one thing that all deserts have in common is that they are very dry. Desert areas not only get little rainfall, under 10 inches (25 centimeters) per year, but also have a rapid evaporation rate due to strong winds and minimal cloud coverage.

Knowing all this, it is remarkable that we find such an astounding variety of plant and animal life thriving in the desert climate, as well as a large number of people. Desert dwellers featured in this section are an Envelopes Camel, a Lappet-faced Vulture Puppet, and a Pecking Woodpecker. Desert plant life is represented by the Expanding Cactus Puppet.

I hope the projects in this section will inspire you to find out more about the fascinating life forms found in the deserts. The list of suggested books on page 152 would be a good starting point.

Expanding Cactus Puppet

Here is what you need:

water
plastic margarine tub
teaspoon
green food coloring
adult-size sock with a ribbed cuff
Styrofoam tray for drying
small round oatmeal box
scissors
white tissue paper
yellow tissue paper
white glue

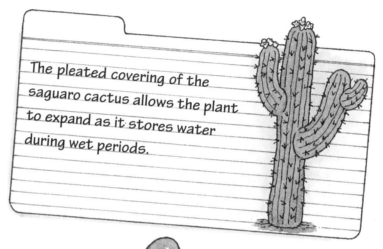

The pleated covering of the saguaro cactus allows the plant to expand as it stores water during wet periods.

Here is what you do:

Put ½ cup (118 ml) of water in the plastic tub. Color the water with a teaspoon of green food coloring. Hold the sock by the toe and dip it into the green water to dye the sock. The sock will suck up most of the colored water. Squeeze out the excess green water and put the sock on the Styrofoam tray to dry.

After it has dried, turn the sock inside out. Tie the foot into a knot. Turn the sock right side out again so the toe now forms the rounded top of the cactus.

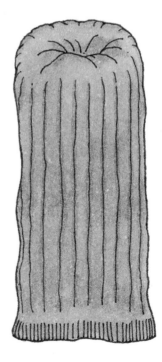

3 Cut the top rim out of the oatmeal box. Cut down the side of the box and cut the bottom out.

4 Wrap the sides of the box around itself to make a small tube. Put the tube inside the cuff of the sock to form the stem of the cactus.

5 Cut the flowers for the cactus from the white tissue paper. Cut a center for each flower from the yellow tissue paper. Glue the flowers to the top of the cactus.

To expand the cactus, just put your hand inside the puppet and push out on the cardboard. The pleats in the cactus will stretch out just the way a real cactus does when it absorbs water in the desert.

131

Pecking Woodpecker

Here is what you need:

ruler
markers
white construction paper
scissors
12-inch by 12-inch (30-cm) square of corrugated
    cardboard
green poster paint
paintbrush
paper fastener
stapler
white glue
uncooked brown rice

The gila woodpecker likes to make its home in the saguaro cactus.

Here is what you do:

Use the markers to draw a 3-inch (8-cm)-high gila woodpecker on the white construction paper. Cut the bird out.

To make the cactus, paint half of the bumpy side of the corrugated cardboard green.

Cut a hole in the center of the green-painted section of the cardboard that is about 3 inches (8 cm) high and 2 inches (5 cm) wide.

4 Attach the bird to the bottom side of the hole with a paper fastener so that it can move back and forth like it is pecking the hole in the cactus.

5 Roll the cardboard into a cactus shape with the green on the outside and the brown part showing through the hole to look like the inside of the cactus. Staple the ends at the top and the bottom to hold them in place.

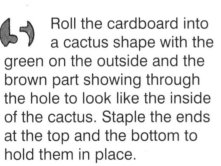

6 Paint the cactus with white glue and sprinkle it with brown rice to look like the spines of the cactus.

The sharp spines of the cactus keep the gila woodpecker safe from predators.

133

Elf Owl Puppet

Here is what you need:

green poster paint
paintbrush
12-inch by 12-inch (30-cm) square of
    corrugated cardboard
ruler
scissors
stapler
brown sock
yellow and black construction paper
    scraps
white glue
orange construction paper scraps

The tiny elf owl also likes to make its home in the saguaro cactus.

Here is what you do:

Paint the bumpy side of the corrugated cardboard green for the outside of the cactus.

When the paint has dried, cut a 3-inch by 4-inch (8-cm by 10-cm) hole in the center of the cardboard. Fold the cardboard into a cylinder shape and staple the ends to hold them in place.

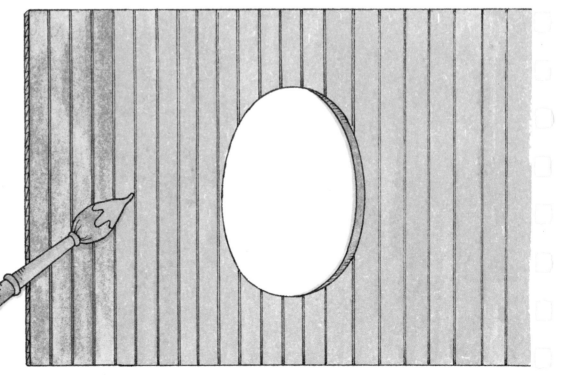

Cut the foot off the brown sock. This will be the owl puppet.

Cut eyes for the owl from the yellow and black paper. Glue the eyes on one side of the sock owl. Cut a beak from orange paper and glue it in place below the eyes.

Put the owl up inside the cactus so that it is looking out the hole. Staple the bottom front of the sock owl to the base of the cactus.

To use your owl puppet, just put your hand up inside the sock and make the owl's head stick out of the cactus as if it is having a look around.

Bottle Peccary

Here is what you need:

scissors
pair of dark brown or black panty hose
gallon-size bleach bottle, thoroughly
    washed and dried
fiberfill
ruler
blue glue gel
masking tape
two flat black buttons
four yellow map pins
four corks that are the same height

The peccary likes to dine on cactus, including the spines!

Here is what you do:

1. Cut one leg off the panty hose. Cut off the foot and knot one of the open ends to close it.

2. Put the bleach bottle, bottom end first, with the lid screwed on, all the way into the stocking. Stuff the fiberfill under the open end of the handle to fill in the space. Knot the open end of the panty hose over the lid of the bottle to hold the fiberfill in place. Trim off any extra stocking.

3. Cut the second leg off the panty hose. Cut off the foot and knot one end of the stocking to close it. Trim off any extra stocking.

4. Put the covered bottle into the stocking, lid end first.

5. Knot the open end of the stocking at the bottom center of the bottle. Trim the excess stocking leaving about 3 inches (7½ cm) for the peccary's tail.

136

6 To make ears, tie a knot in the foot trimmed from each stocking, about 2 inches (5 cm) from the toe. Trim off any excess stocking. Turn the covered bottle on its side with the handle on top. Glue an ear on each side of the handle.

7 Put a small piece of masking tape on the back of each button to make a better gluing surface. Glue a button about halfway down and on each side of the handle. Put a yellow map pin through one end of the holes in each button to make a pupil.

8 Dip the other two map pins in glue and slip them into the stocking and fiberfill at the lid end of the handle to make the nostrils.

9 Glue the corks on the bottom of the peccary (the side of the bottle) for legs.

Keep a close eye on this fellow. Within hours of being born, a peccary can outrun a person!

Jackrabbit Marionette

Here is what you need:

four paper-towel tubes
stapler
ruler
scissors
masking tape
cereal-box cardboard
white glue
pink poster paint
paintbrush
brown poster paint
newspaper to work on
1½ to 2-inch (4- to 5-cm) large black
    pom-pom
two wiggle eyes
fiberfill
yarn
hole punch
toilet-tissue tube

The large feet of the jackrabbit enable it to run very fast.

Here is what you do:

To make each ear, flatten a paper-towel tube and fold the sides of one end inside itself to make the pointed top of the ear. Fold the bottom of the tube in half to give the ear dimension. Staple the bottom to hold the fold in place.

Cut an 8-inch (20-cm) slit up each side of another paper-towel tube and cut across to remove the top piece from the tube. The uncut front portion of the tube will be the head of the rabbit. Staple one ear on each side of the tube just behind the head.

138

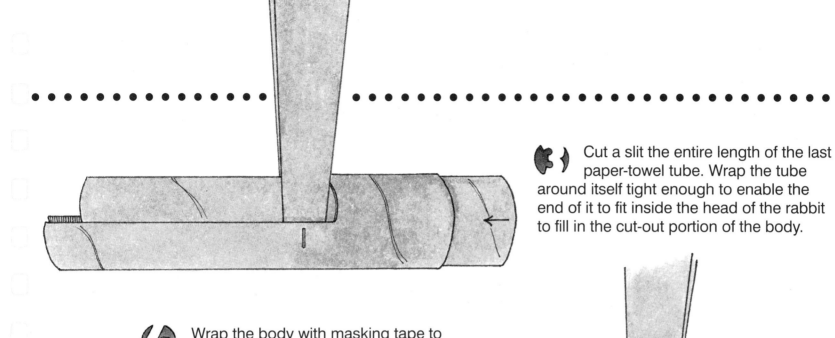

3 Cut a slit the entire length of the last paper-towel tube. Wrap the tube around itself tight enough to enable the end of it to fit inside the head of the rabbit to fill in the cut-out portion of the body.

4 Wrap the body with masking tape to hold the tubes together and in place.

5 Cut front and back legs for the rabbit from the cardboard. Glue the legs on each side of the body. You may need to use masking tape to hold them in place while the glue dries.

6 Paint the inside of the rabbit ears pink. Paint the rest of the rabbit a light brown.

7 Glue the black pom-pom in the opening at the head of the rabbit for a nose. Glue the two wiggle eyes on the head. Glue a puff of fiberfill in the opening at the rear of the rabbit for a tail. (If you wish to make a black-tailed jackrabbit, you will need to color the fiberfill tail with black paint.)

8 Cut a 5-foot (152-cm) piece of yarn. Punch a hole in the tip of each ear. String the yarn through each hole and through the toilet-tissue tube, then tie the two ends of the yarn together.

Hold onto the small tube and hop your jackrabbit along the ground.

Envelopes Camel Puppet

Here is what you need:

brown construction paper
scissors
white glue
black marker
two identical brown greeting-card envelopes
    (you may need to color white ones)

Here is what you do:

Cut four legs, a tail, a head, and two ears for the camel from the brown construction paper.

Glue the two ears on the head. Draw a face for the camel with the black marker.

Open the flaps of the two envelopes. Hold the backs of the two envelopes together with the flaps open. Glue the edges of the two sides and flaps of the envelope together, leaving the bottom open. The flaps of the envelopes will form the two sides of the hump of the camel.

While the glue is still wet, slip the head between the glued envelopes on one side, and the tail on the other.

Glue a front and back leg on each side of the envelopes.

The dromedary camel has only one hump.

To use the camel puppet, just slip your hand between the two envelopes at the bottom and take this "ship of the desert" for a walk.

141

Coyote Paper Keeper

Here is what you need:

cereal box
scissors
newspaper to work on
yellow poster paint
paintbrush
pencil
brown construction paper
white glue
black marker

While coyotes are able to survive in a variety of climates, they are often associated with American desert areas.

Here is what you do:

1) Cut the box into two triangle-shaped pieces by cutting from the bottom corner to the opposite corner at the top of the box. You will use the bottom triangle of the box for the body of the coyote.

2) Paint the inside of the box yellow and let it dry.

3) Trace around the two triangle sides of the box on the brown paper and cut the triangles out.

4) Trace around the bottom and the side edge of the box on the brown paper. Cut the shape out leaving about ½-inch (1 cm) of extra paper on each side of the tracing.

(5) Glue the paper to the two sides of the box, folding the extra paper over on both sides. Trim off any paper that overhangs the edges of the box.

(6) Glue the two brown paper triangles over each side of the box so that the outside of the box is completely covered with brown paper.

(7) Cut a tail for the coyote from brown paper. Use scissors to fringe around the edge of the tail. Glue the edge of the tail to the bottom of the box so that it sticks out from the open side.

(8) Use the black marker to draw, on both sides of the box, the face and legs of a sitting coyote with its head pointed up howling.

(9) Cut two ears from the brown paper. Glue an ear on each side of the head of the coyote.

This howling coyote will be glad to sit on your desk to hold important papers and letters.

Oasis Stamp Licker

Here is what you need:

2 brown 12-inch (30-cm) pipe cleaners
2 green 12-inch (30-cm) pipe cleaners
plaster of paris mix
water
small plastic margarine tub
newspaper
blue sponge
ruler
scissors
white glue
sand

An oasis is an area of the desert that has a steady supply of water.

Here is what you do:

Make a palm tree by folding the two brown pipe cleaners in half and twisting them together to form the trunk of the tree. Use the green pipe cleaners to shape palm leaves for the tree. Slide the ends of the palm-leaves pipe cleaners through the folded end of the tree-trunk pipe cleaners to attach them.

Mix the plaster in the margarine tub according to the package directions. The tub should be about three quarters full of plaster.

3) Cut a 2-inch (5-cm) circle from the blue sponge. Before the plaster has set, press the sponge into the center of the tub until the top of the sponge is level with the plaster.

4) Press the base of the palm tree into the wet plaster beside the sponge "water."

5) Let the plaster set completely, then remove the plaster shape from the tub.

6) Cover the top of the plaster around the sponge water with white glue, then sprinkle it with sand. Let the glue dry.

To use the oasis stamp licker just moisten the sponge with water and rub stamps across the sponge to wet them.

Tortoise Treasure Keeper

Here is what you need:

small tuna-fish-type can
masking tape
yellow-colored craft glue
about twenty-five buttons in shades of brown
corrugated cardboard
pen
felt
scissors
jar lid small enough to fit under the can
white glue

The slow-moving tortoise can go for long periods of time in the desert without eating or drinking.

Here is what you do:

1. Invert the can to form a shell for the tortoise. Cover the bottom of the can (now the top of the tortoise shell) with masking tape to create a better gluing surface.

2. Cover the masking tape with the yellow glue. Arrange as many buttons as you need on top of the glue to cover the top of the tortoise shell.

3. Place the can on the corrugated cardboard. Sketch the head, legs, and tail of a tortoise coming out from the shell. Cut the tortoise shape out.

Cut a circle of felt to fit inside the jar lid. Put a piece of masking tape in the lid and on one side of the felt circle to create better gluing surfaces. Glue the felt inside the lid, tape side down, with the white glue.

Put a piece of tape on the outside (top) of the lid. Use the white glue to attach the lid to the center of the tortoise shape for a little dish in which to keep small treasures.

Use white glue to attach two buttons to the head of the tortoise for eyes.

Put your tiny treasures in the felt-lined lid and cover them with the can shell of the tortoise to hide them. No one will ever suspect your tortoise has a secret compartment!

Palmate Gecko Magnet

Here is what you need:

two 12-inch (30-cm) brown pipe cleaners
ruler
scissors
white glue
wooden ice-cream spoon
masking tape
Styrofoam tray for drying
facial tissue
yellow-colored glue
sticky-back magnet strip
brown marker
two small black beads

The webbed feet of the palmate gecko are not for moving through water, but through the desert sand.

Here is what you do:

1. Cut one of the brown pipe cleaners in half to use for the front and back legs of the gecko. Cut a 4-inch (10-cm) piece from the second pipe cleaner for the tail.

2. Rub glue all over one side of the spoon. Lay the front and back legs across the spoon so that they stick out on each side. Lay the tail along the spoon so that it sticks out the small handle end of the spoon, which will be the back of the gecko. Secure the pipe cleaners with more glue and masking tape and let the glue dry.

3. When the glue has dried, shape knees and feet on the legs of the gecko. Make the front legs shorter than the back legs by trimming them. Cut the remaining piece of pipe cleaner into eight 1-inch (2.5-cm) pieces. Wrap two pieces around each foot to make five toes—one will be formed by the end of the leg pipe cleaner and the other four by the two ends of each piece you wrap around the foot.

4. Cut squares of facial tissue large enough to wrap over each foot. Glue a tissue square over each foot using the yellow-colored glue.

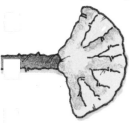

5. When the glue has dried, put a piece of sticky-back magnet on each foot.

6. Use the marker to color the top of the gecko brown. Use the yellow glue to dab a strip of color down the back of the gecko.

7. Glue on the two black beads for eyes.

Stick your gecko to the refrigerator. A real gecko really can climb up the wall with no problem, so I guess it could climb up a refrigerator too!

Lappet-faced Vulture Puppet

Here is what you need:

newspaper to work on
black poster paint
paintbrush
four 9-inch (23-cm) uncoated paper
 plates
scissors
red construction paper
black marker
yellow construction paper
white glue
stapler
12-inch (30-cm) black pipe cleaner

Here is what you do:

Paint the bottom side of three of the paper plates black. Let the plates dry.

Cut an oval-shaped head for the vulture from the red paper. Use the marker to draw two eyes on the head. Cut a beak from the yellow paper and glue it in place below the eyes.

The lappet-faced vulture is a scavenger. It keeps the desert clean by eating dead animals.

3) Staple the head to one end of the black pipe cleaner. Staple the other end of the pipe cleaner to the back of one of the black painted plates so that the plate forms a body and the pipe cleaner forms a neck that comes up over the body to give the vulture its typical hunched-over look.

4) Cut the last paper plate in half. Staple a half plate across the back of the body plate over the end of the pipe cleaner forming the neck. This will make a place for your hand to slide into the vulture puppet.

5) Fold one black plate over each side of the body to make wings for the vulture. Staple the wings in place.

Fly your vulture around to see if it can spot a meal. YUK!

Books About Deserts

Albert, Richard E. *Alejandro's Gift.* San Francisco: Chronicle Books, 1994.

Arnold, Caroline. *A Walk in the Desert.* Parsippany, NJ: Silver Press, 1990.

Cloudsley-Thompson, John Leonard. *Animals of the Desert.* New York: McGraw-Hill, 1971.

Flanagan, Alice. *Desert Birds.* Danbury, CT: Children's Press, 1996.

Gibson, Barbara. *Creatures of the Desert World*. Washington, D.C.: National Geographic Society, 1987.

Greenaway, Frank. *Desert Life.* New York: Dorling Kindersley, 1992.

Hirschi, Ron. *Desert.* New York: Bantam Books, 1992.

Macquity, Miranda. *Desert.* New York: Alfred A. Knopf, 1994.

Savage, Stephen. *Animals of the Desert.* Austin, TX: Raintree Steck-Vaughn Publishers, 1997.

Spencer, Guy. *A Living Desert.* Mahwah, NJ: Troll Associates, 1988.

Taylor, Bradford. *Desert Life.* London: Dorling Kindersley, 1992.

Twist, Clint. *Deserts.* New York: Dillon Press, 1991.

Wallace, Marianne D. *America's Deserts.* Golden, CO: Fulcrum Kids, 1996.

Weiwandt, Thomas. *The Hidden Life of the Desert.* New York: Crown Publishers, 1990.

Wright-Frierson, Virginia. *A Desert Scrapbook: Dawn to Dusk in the Sonoran Desert.* New York: Simon and Schuster Books for Young Readers, 1996.

Reptiles

There are four groups of reptiles left in the world today—turtles and tortoises, snakes and lizards, crocodilian, and all by itself, the tuatara. All reptiles are cold-blooded. This means that body temperature is not constant, but depends on the outside environment of the animals. While the appearance of reptiles vary, they all are covered with scales. Reptiles need air to breathe.

This section features models of a Head of a Threatened Horn Toad (did you know it shoots blood from its eyes when irritated?), a Bag Komodo Dragon, and a Licking Gecko. If you do not already have one or more books with colorful pictures of reptiles, I recommend that you go to the library and take some out. I've suggested a few of the more interesting ones on page 175. The books will give you a clearer picture of what each animal actually looks like before you attempt to make it, and you'll also pick up lots of entertaining and interesting information about these amazing creatures.

Paper Plate Chameleon

Here is what you need:

two paper plates
yellow pipe cleaner, 12 inches (30 cm) long
stapler
scissors
two cone-shaped party hats
two cloves
white glue
paintbrush and green and yellow poster paints
newspaper to work on
Styrofoam tray for drying

Here is what you do:

Fold one paper plate in half and staple it together at the top edge to hold the fold. This will be the body of the chameleon.

Fold the second plate in half and cut a pie-shaped wedge from it, with the fold, the cut, and the fluted edge of the plate all about 3½ inches (9 cm) long. This will be the head of the chameleon. Slide the folded piece partway over one end of the plate body and staple it in place so that the fold in the body forms an open mouth.

Cut four 5-inch (12.5-cm) legs from the fluted edge of the second paper plate. Staple a leg on each side of the front of the chameleon behind the head. Staple the other two legs toward the back of the chameleon, one on each side.

154

4 Cut a long, curly tail from the center portion of the second paper plate. Staple the tail, curving down and under, between the folds at the back of the body.

5 Cut a 1-inch (2.5-cm) tip from the end of each party hat for the cone-shaped eyes of the chameleon. Glue one on each side of the head. (You can paint the tip of a cone-shaped paper cup instead.)

6 Paint the chameleon with green and yellow poster paint—or another color. Chameleons are known for their ability to change color to blend in with their surroundings. Decide where you are going to display your chameleon and paint it the same color as its background. Let the chameleon dry on the Styrofoam tray.

7 Dip the stems of two cloves into glue and then slip them onto the top of the eye cones. A real chameleon has eyes that can actually swivel around to look in different directions.

8 Dip the end of the yellow pipe cleaner in the glue, then slide it partway into the mouth. Leave most of the pipe cleaner sticking out for the amazingly long tongue.

You might want to make a small paper bug to glue on the tip of this hungry reptile's tongue.

Head of a Threatened Horned Toad

Here is what you need:

old adult-size brown sock
two tops with pull-up spouts from dish detergent
   bottles
red pipe cleaners
black permanent marker
scissors
masking tape
rubber band

Here is what you do:

Cut the foot off the brown sock. Cut a ½-inch (1¼ -cm) slit across each side of the toe end of the sock.

Use the black permanent marker to color the spouts of the two detergent bottle tops. Tape the two spouts together, side by side, to form the two eyes for the horned toad. Slip the eyes inside the sock foot and work one spout through each of the cuts in the toe end of the sock. The black spouts should now be sticking out of the sock to look like two eyes.

The horned toad is actually a lizard, not a toad. When threatened, it will confuse and startle its enemies by squirting blood from its eyelids.

3 Cut 2-inch (5-cm) spikes around the cuff of the top piece of sock. Slide the spiky sock over the foot piece so that the spikes at the head end stick out past the eyes. Hold the spiky sock in place around the eye caps with a rubber band. Fold the cut spikes back over the rubber band so that they stick out around the eyes to resemble the head of the spiky little horned toad.

4 Cut two 4-inch (10-cm) pieces of red pipe cleaner. Pull both eye spouts out to open them all the way. Slide one piece of red pipe cleaner down into each eye cap. Reach inside the sock puppet and pull each pipe cleaner down into the sock until the end is level with the opening in the spout. Dot the tip of the pipe cleaner with the black marker.

To use the puppet, just put your hand inside and push on the ends of the two pipe cleaners to make them come out of the eyes like squirting blood. The pipe cleaners weaken very quickly with use, so if your horned toad is easily threatened, it would be a good idea to have extra red pipe cleaners on hand for reloading.

Hissing Tuatara

Here is what you need:

empty soda can, washed and dried completely
a tablespoon of sand
aluminum foil
masking tape
two cats'-eye marbles
brown tissue paper
white glue
plastic margarine tub for mixing
Styrofoam tray for drying
newspaper to work on

The tuatara is the only living member of its order of reptiles, the rest of which died out millions of years ago. That is why the tuatara is called a "living fossil."

Here is what you do:

1 Put about a tablespoon of sand into the soda can. Seal the opening of the can with masking tape.

2 Tear off a piece of aluminum foil 2 feet (61 cm) long. Wrap the foil around the can with about 4 inches (10 cm) of the foil sticking out from the top of the can to shape into a head. Squeeze the excess foil sticking out from the bottom of the can into a band that comes to a point for the tail of the tuatara.

3 Tear off another piece of foil about 6 inches (15 cm) long. Squeeze the foil into a strip for the front legs and feet of the tuatara. Shape five clawed toes at the end of each foot. Repeat to make the back legs.

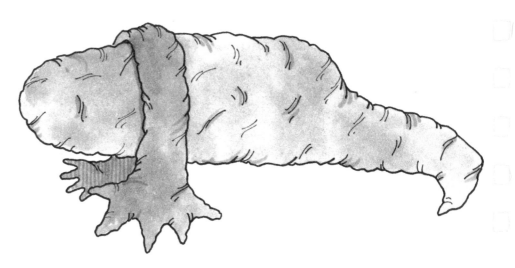

158

5 Pinch a crest up from the foil on the back of the tuatara, starting behind the head and running down the back to the end of the tail.

6 Mix two parts glue with one part water in a margarine tub. Dip pieces of brown tissue into the watery glue and use them to cover the entire tuatara. Push the foil claws through the tissue to make them stand out.

7 Use your fingers to push an eye socket into the foil on each side of the head. Glue a small piece of masking tape into each socket and onto each marble to create better gluing surfaces. Glue a marble in each hole for eyes.

4 Bend the two sets of legs over the back of the tuatara so that there are front and back feet on each side. Use masking tape to hold the leg strips in place.

When the glue has dried, shake your tuatara and listen to it hiss.

Licking Gecko

Here is what you need:

green construction paper
pencil
bubble wrap with small bubbles
two flat buttons
masking tape
old red or pink glove
white glue
stapler
scissors

The gecko has no eyelids, so it must use its long tongue to keep its eyes moist.

Here is what you do:

Draw the outline of the top view of the gecko on the green paper. Cut out the outline.

Staple a piece of bubble wrap, flat side down, over the lizard. Trim the bubble wrap to fit, then add more staples around the outside of the lizard to hold it in place.

160

3 Glue the two buttons to the head of the lizard for eyes. Put a piece of masking tape on the bubble wrap where you want to glue each eye. This will create an area the glue will stick to.

4 Cut a finger from the glove to make a tongue for the puppet. Use masking tape to tape the open end of the tongue under one side of the head. You should place the tongue so that when you slip your finger in it, you can curl it up to lick the eyes of the gecko. When you have the tongue properly placed, use the stapler to secure it.

Geckos come in a variety of colors and patterns. You might want to make your gecko a different color.

Bag Komodo Dragon

The biggest lizard in the world is the Komodo dragon.

Here is what you need:

five large brown paper grocery bags
paper-towel tube
paintbrush and white, pink, and black poster paint
bubble wrap with small bubbles
masking tape
white glue
newspaper for stuffing and to work on
black marker
crinkle-cut scissors

Here is what you do:

1. Open two bags and stuff them almost to the top with crumpled newspaper. Slide the opening of one bag over the opening of the other and glue them together. This will be the body of the Komodo dragon.

2. To make the head, use crinkle-cut scissors to cut the bottom out of a bag. Cut a triangle-shaped piece out of each side of the bag so that the opening looks like a mouth with sharp teeth. Slide the top of the bag over one end of the body and glue it in place.

3. Cut the paper-towel tube in half and use one half to make a tongue. Cut a fork in one end of the tongue. Glue the other end in the bottom back of the mouth between the two bags.

162

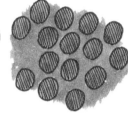

4 Slide the opening of an empty bag over the back of the body and glue it in place.

5 Flatten out the last bag. Fold the bottom of the bag into a point and glue it in place. Use masking tape to help hold the folds. This will be the tip of the tail. Glue the opening of the tail to the bottom of the last bag. The folded part of the tail should be facing down so that the top is smooth.

6 To give the lizard a scaly look, print the entire body using bubble wrap: Paint over a piece of wrap with black paint and print the bubble shapes on the lizard. Keep repainting the bubbles until you have printed the entire body.

7 Paint the inside of the mouth pale pink. Give the tongue a thick coating of white paint. Use the black marker to draw eyes on the top of the head and crouching legs on each side of the body.

Real Komodo dragons can be up to 10 feet (3 m) long. If you want your dragon to be longer, just add more stuffed bags to its middle.

163

Shedding Snake

Here is what you need:

a long white sock, such as a woman's knee sock
red pipe cleaner, 12 inches (30 cm) long
black permanent marker
white glue
scissors
paintbrush and green poster paint
fiberfill
rubber band
old pair of pantyhose
newspaper to work on
Styrofoam tray for drying

A snake will outgrow and shed its skin many times during its lifetime.

Here is what you do:

To make the snake, stuff the entire sock with fiberfill. Close the open end of the sock with a rubber band. This will be the tail end of the snake.

Paint the entire snake with green paint.

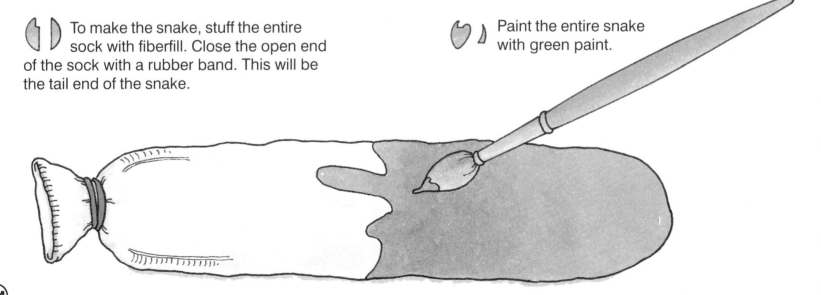

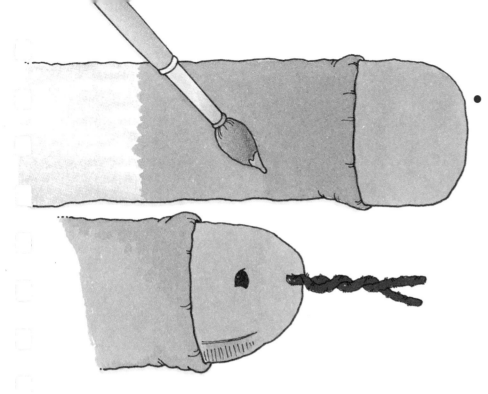

3) Cut off one leg of the pantyhose. Starting at the tail of the snake, pull the stocking leg over the entire snake for the skin. Paint the stocking green while it is over the snake, and let it dry.

4) Fold the red pipe cleaner in half and twist it together with the ends spread slightly apart to make the forked tongue. Cut a tiny hole in the toe end of the sock. Dip the folded end of the pipe cleaner in glue and stick it in the hole so that the tongue is sticking out of the head.

5) Use the marker to draw eyes on the head of the snake. You can draw eyes on the skin over the head, too.

To shed its skin, a snake will rub its head against something rough and continue rubbing until it slips totally out of the old skin. Try this with your snake.

In and Out Red-eared Terrapin

Here is what you need:

small paper bowl
cereal box cardboard
four wooden ice-cream spoons
two craft sticks
small sliding matchbox
masking tape
scissors
stapler
a few strands of dry spaghetti
black marker
paintbrush and brown, yellow, and red poster paint
white glue
newspaper to work on
Styrofoam tray for drying

Here is what you do:

1. Trace around the rim of the bowl on the cardboard. Cut out the circle. The upside-down bowl will be the top shell of the turtle, and the cardboard circle will be the bottom shell.

2. Glue the four wooden spoons to the print side of the cardboard circle so that they stick out for the legs of the turtle. Glue the craft stick on the edge of the circle so that it sticks out for the tail. Use masking tape to help secure the glued sticks.

The red-eared terrapin is easy to recognize. It has a red stripe along each side of its head.

3. Staple the upside-down bowl over the cardboard circle so that the legs and tail stick out from the sides.

4 Paint the entire turtle brown, then dab some yellow on the shell. Slide the inner box out of the matchbox and paint the short sides and bottom brown with dabs of yellow. Paint the two long sides red for the band of color on each side of the terrapin's head. Let the project dry.

5 Glue the outer box of the matchbox on the bottom edge of the turtle where the head should come out. Use masking tape to hold it in place while the glue dries.

6 Cut a slit along the bottom of one of the short sides of the inner box. Slide the end of a craft stick into the slit and glue it to the bottom of the box. Use masking tape to hold it in place.

7 Slide the inner box, stick first, into the outer box under the shell so that the stick is hidden under the turtle. By pushing and pulling on the stick, you can make the turtle's head go in and out. Use a black marker to draw eyes on the turtle head.

8 Break off tiny pieces of spaghetti and glue five to the end of each leg forclaws.

This red-eared terrapin can move its head in and out of its shell just like a real one can.

Mother Crocodile

Here is what you need:

long cardboard gift-wrap tube about 1½ inches
    (4 cm) across
cardboard paper-towel tube
cereal box cardboard
two cotton balls
masking tape
dark color paper scrap
white glue
scissors
crinkle-cut scissors
paintbrush and red, white, brown, and green poster
    paint
newspaper to work on

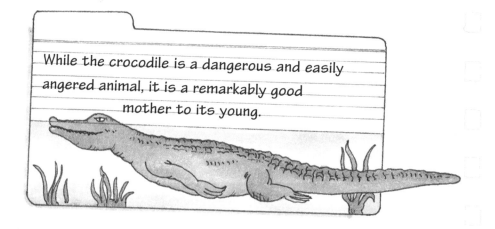

While the crocodile is a dangerous and easily angered animal, it is a remarkably good mother to its young.

Here is what you do:

Cut a slit halfway up the paper-towel tube. Wrap the cut end of the tube around itself to form a pointed tail. Hold the wrapped tube in place with masking tape. Glue the uncut end of the tube into one end of the longer tube, which will form the crocodile's body and head. Use crinkle-cut scissors to cut a mouth for the crocodile from the head end of the wrapping-paper tube. Cut a jagged slit about 8 inches (20 cm) long out of each side to look like an open mouth full of teeth.

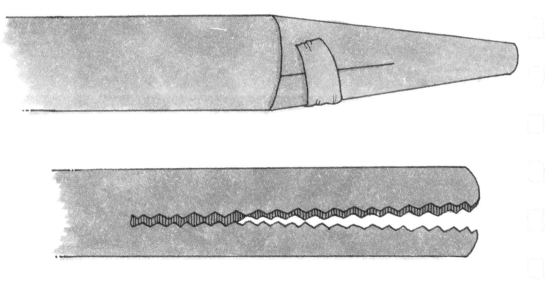

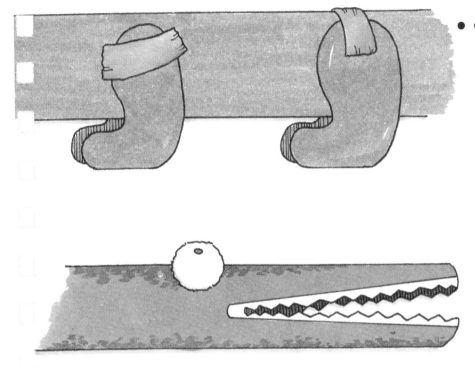

Cut four legs from the cardboard. Glue two on each side of the body portion of the crocodile. Use masking tape to help hold them in place.

If you wish to make your crocodile look scaly, you can cover the body with torn pieces of masking tape.

Paint the inside of the mouth red, the teeth white, and the rest of the crocodile a green and brown color.

Glue two cotton balls above the cut jaws of the crocodile for eyes. Cut pupils from scrap paper and glue them in place.

You might want to color and cut out some baby crocodiles to ride around in your mother crocodile's mouth.

Clothespin Alligator

Here is what you need:

three spring-type wooden clothespins
pipe cleaner, 6 inches (15 cm) long
two large wiggle eyes
paintbrush and yellow and green poster paint
white glue
scissors
newspaper to work on

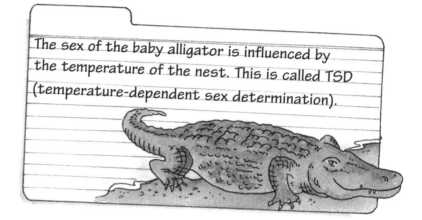

The sex of the baby alligator is influenced by the temperature of the nest. This is called TSD (temperature-dependent sex determination).

Here is what you do:

Hold one clothespin open. Pinch a second clothespin over the top of the open clothespin and glue it in place. This will be the head of the alligator, and the first clothespin will be the body.

To make the tail, attach the third clothespin to the back top of the first clothespin and glue it in place.

3) Cut the pipe cleaner into two pieces. Slide one piece through the body clothespin toward the front to form front legs on each side. Bend the legs down and bend the ends forward to shape feet. Slide the second piece of pipe cleaner between the top end of the body clothespin and the tail for back legs. Shape legs and feet as you did with the front legs.

Don't worry about the open mouth. That is how an alligator cools off.

4) Paint the inside of the alligator's mouth pale yellow. Paint the rest of the alligator, including the legs, green.

5) Glue a wiggle eye to each side of the alligator's head.

171

Alligator Snapping Turtle Puppet

Here is what you need:

four 9-inch (23-cm) paper plates
two long white socks
elbow macaroni
two flat black buttons
stapler
white glue
scissors
old tennis ball
piece of pink or red pipe cleaner
paintbrush and brown, white, and red poster paint
old glove
two small wiggle eyes
newspaper to work on

The alligator snapping turtle has a wormlike appendage in the bottom of its mouth to lure its dinner right between its powerful jaws.

Here is what you do:

Ask an adult to cut a slit across an old tennis ball using a sharp knife. Put the ball, cut end first, down in the toe of one of the socks. This will be the head of the alligator turtle. Push the end of the sock into the slit in the tennis ball to form a mouth for the turtle.

Cut the cuff end of the long sock that the head is in into a point to form the tail of the turtle.

Cut the foot off the second sock. Flatten the foot portion so that the bottom of the sock is underneath. Cut the foot into four equal pieces for the legs of the turtle.

4 Arrange the legs on the rim of the eating side of a paper plate. Set another plate, eating side up, on top of the first plate and staple the plates together at the legs to hold them in place. This will be the bottom shell of the turtle.

5 Staple two more plates together to make the top shell. Staple the plates, bottom side up, on each side of the bottom shell so that you can fit your hand and arm in between the top and bottom shells.

6 Paint the top and bottom shells and the legs brown. Paint the head and the tail of the turtle brown. Paint the inside of the turtle's mouth a reddish pink color. Use the white paint to lighten the red paint a little.

7 Glue five macaroni claws on the end of each leg.

Poke a piece of pipe cleaner into the bottom of the turtle's mouth to make the wormlike appendage. Glue the buttons above the mouth to make eyes. Slide the head between the top and bottom shells so that the head sticks out one end and the tail out the other end.

Make a tiny fish for the turtle to catch by cutting a finger from an old glove and gluing two wiggle eyes on the tip.

To use your alligator snapping turtle, place your hand into the head sock and put your fingers on each side of the cut tennis ball. By squeezing the ball on each side, the mouth of the turtle will open and the appendage will wiggle. Put the fish on a finger of your other hand, and show how the turtle catches dinner.

Books About Reptiles

Bender, Lionel. *Fish to Reptiles*. New York: Gloucester Press, 1988.

Caitlin, Stephen. *Discovering Reptiles and Amphibians*. Mahwah, NJ: Troll Associates, 1990.

Chatfield, June. *A Look Inside Reptiles.* Pleasantville, NY: Reader's Digest Young Families, 1995.

Chermayeff, Ivan. *Scaly Facts.* San Diego, CA: Harcourt Brace, 1995.

Creagh, Carson. *Reptiles.* Alexandria, VA: Time-Life Books, 1996.

Elliott, Leslee. *Really Radical Reptiles and Amphibians.* New York, NY: Sterling, 1994.

Heller, Ruth. *Ruth Heller's How to Hide a Crocodile & Other Reptiles.* New York: Grosset & Dunlap, 1994.

Ling, Mary. *Amazing Crocodiles and Reptiles.* New York: Knopf, 1991.

Llamas Ruiz, Andres. *Reptiles and Amphibians: Birth and Growth.* New York: Sterling, 1996.

Parker, Steve. *Revolting Reptiles.* Austin, TX: Raintree Steck-Vaughn, 1994.

Retan, Walter. *101 Wacky Facts About Snakes & Reptiles.* New York, NY: Scholastic, 1991.

Ricciuti, Edward R. *Reptiles.* Woodbridge, CT: Blackbirch Press, 1993.

Richardson, Joy. *Reptiles.* New York: Franklin Watts, 1993.

Roberts, M. L. *World's Weirdest Reptiles.* Mahwah, NJ: Watermill Press, 1994.

Spinelli, Eileen. *Reptiles*. Lincolnwood, IL: Publications International, Ltd., 1991.

Stonehouse, Bernard. *A Closer Look at Reptiles.* New York: Gloucester Press, 1979.

Tesar, Jenny E. *What on Earth Is a Tuatara?* Woodbridge, CT: Blackbirch Press, 1994.

Wise, William. *Giant Snakes and Other Amazing Reptiles.* New York: Putnam, 1970.

Index